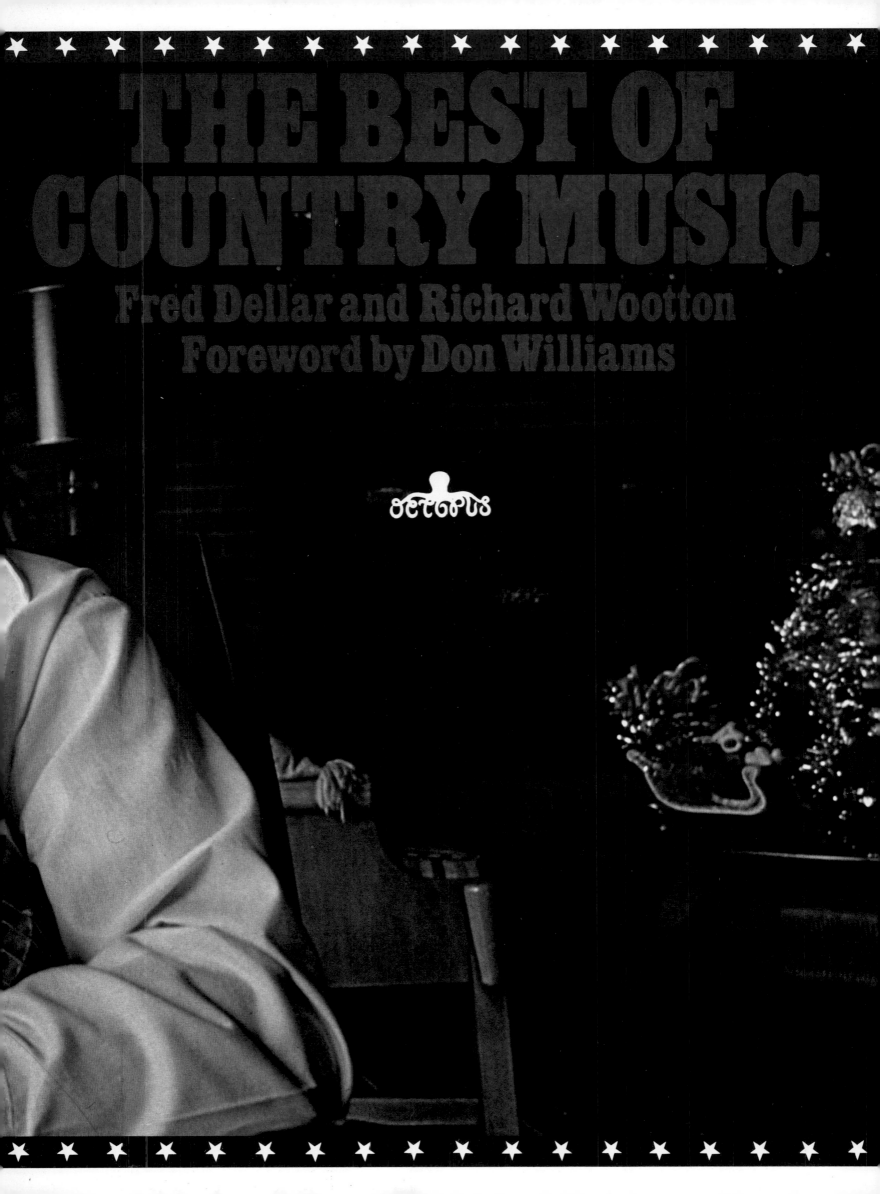

THE BEST OF
COUNTRY MUSIC

Fred Dellar and Richard Wootton
Foreword by Don Williams

First published in 1980 by
Octopus Books Limited
59 Grosvenor Street
London W1

© 1980 Octopus Books Limited

ISBN 0 7064 1204 4

Produced by Mandarin Publishers Limited
22A Westlands Road,
Quarry Bay, Hong Kong

Printed in Hong Kong

CONTENTS

FOREWORD

Any book that encourages the love of country music is all right by me –
especially one like this, which doesn't preach that any particular aspect
is the way things ought to be.

Old-time, gospel, blues, western swing, cajun, bluegrass, mainstream, country-pop, country-rock, they're all part of the whole we know
as country music. And though I'm not keen on labels – why does music
have to have labels? – I guess that they do serve to remind folks that
country is not just Bill Monroe playing *Blue Moon Of Kentucky*, Bob Wills
swingin' through a version of *Ida Red*, Waylon 'n' Willie singing about
Texas, or even me reprising *Shelter Of Your Eyes* in answer to a request
– diverse as these performances may be.

For country music is a lot of sounds, a lot of things and a lot of people
and *The Best Of Country Music*, through its words and pictures,
explains as much in a way that anyone – even a non-believer – will
understand. Which is why I tip my hat to it.

Don Williams

page 1: *Dolly Parton*
page 2/3: *Roy Acuff*
page 4/5: *Johnny Cash*
right: *Don Williams*

right: *By the Seventies country had become the music of the whole country. A major breakthrough came in May 1977 when New York City's world famous Carnegie Hall played host to Don Williams, Roy Clark, Freddy Fender and Hank Thompson for a special* Country In New York *show.*

AT the Lone Star Café, a Texas-style country music venue at Greenwich Village, a packed house of normally sophisticated New Yorkers are dressed in denims, cowboy boots and stetsons and mouthing the words of a song called *Take This Job and Shove It*. The performance by Johnny Paycheck, a one-time Nashville sideman but now a star in his own right, is also being heard by several thousand radio listeners over a live relay on the city's popular country music station WHN.

Across town at the prestigious Carnegie Hall a more smartly dressed audience are watching Crystal Gayle, the glamorous young singer with beautiful straight hair so long she can sit on it, performing one of her hits, *Don't It Make My Brown Eyes Blue*.

The atmosphere at Chicago's Aragon Ballroom, a once-glorious dance palace but now a venue for big-name rock artists, is close to hysteria. A crowd of over five thousand fans are stomping, cheering and shouting encouragement to Willie Nelson, the mild-mannered, hugely popular leader of country music's 'outlaws'. A week later the long-haired Texan, still wearing a T-shirt, jeans, sneakers and a red bandana, will be topping the bill at Caesar's Palace on Las Vegas's glittering 'strip'. The audience, in the town where country music is now featured on a nightly basis side by side with the middle-of-the-road cabaret artists who previously had dominated all the musical venues, will be more restrained but equally enthusiastic.

Next to the TV and film studios at Universal City in Southern California an open-air concert is coming to an end and a vast crowd, ranging from teenagers to senior citizens, are on their feet cheering Kenny Rogers. Nearby, the curvaceous, honey-blonde superstar Dolly Parton has just finished taping a segment for Johnny Carson's nationally networked *Tonight* TV show.

Perhaps these events did not happen the same night, though they could have, but they serve to illustrate the widespread popularity of country music today. It has come a long way from the time when it was only associated with people living in the rural areas of the Southern USA. If you lived in a big sophisticated city and liked country music you tended to hide your records in the closet and smile weakly whenever friends made a prejudiced comment about the music they considered a cliché-ridden genre of nasal vocals and whining steel guitars. Today country music turns up everywhere – on TV, radio and in clubs in every American town and city. In the same way that it has spread across the USA, it is now gaining increasing popularity throughout the world.

Like any living thing country music has never stopped changing and growing. It is no longer possible to categorize it, to talk of a basic way it should sound or of the instruments it should be played on. As Kris Kristofferson says before he sings *Me and Bobby McGee*, 'If it sounds country, man, that's what it is, a country song.'

A majority of the most popular singers in country music today have made records in a pop vein and have been successful with easy-listening or rock audiences. When a country artist deliberately sets out to appeal to non-country fans – and succeeds – they are said to have 'crossed over'. These performers come in for a lot of criticism from purists who argue that they are weakening country music, making it blander, and taking it to the point where it will eventually become indistinguishable from pop.

COUNTRY MUSIC TODAY

above: *Glen Campbell – seen here with John Wayne in his Academy Award winning role as the one-eyed US marshal, Rooster Cogburn, in the western* True Grit *– has enjoyed a long and varied career in show business. He has made dozens of country-pop records including his biggest hit* Rhinestone Cowboy *– the song about an ambitious hustler in New York – which topped the country, pop and easy-listening charts in 1977, and he has appeared frequently on network TV and in movies. Born in a rural community, near the tiny Arkansas town of Delight, Glen decided at an early age that music was preferable to farming and travelled around the US taking a variety of jobs including session work with such artists as Jan and Dean, Rick Nelson and Elvis, and a brief spell as a member of The Beach Boys.*

Crossover artists, producers and other interested parties will contend that the music is, and always will be, rooted in country. By adding strings and saxophones they are making their music more accessible to pop fans and therefore reach a wider audience than previously has shown little interest in the music. With success in the pop or rock market-place they can play bigger venues, hire better musicians and produce an altogether more professional show.

The concern of the purists is understandable as many crossover records sound very different from the country music of the past, but it's difficult to argue with success. Contemporary country music is big business and it seems likely that many of the crossover artists will eventually become as established with middle-of-the-road pop audiences as Frank Sinatra, Dean Martin or Tony Bennett.

The crossover phenomenon is a fairly recent one. Country stars of the Fifties and Sixties were usually able to retain their popularity with the country fans for many years. But once they reached the top of their profession they weren't able to go much higher. Artists rarely set out to score with pop fans and success in the charts was usually more by accident than design and often a one-off event. Bill Anderson had one top twenty pop hit (*Still* in 1963), as did Tammy Wynette (with *Stand By Your Man* in 1969) while top country stars like Loretta Lynn have had none.

Things changed in the Seventies when artists like Dolly Parton and Kenny Rogers, with the active help of their record companies and management, deliberately courted

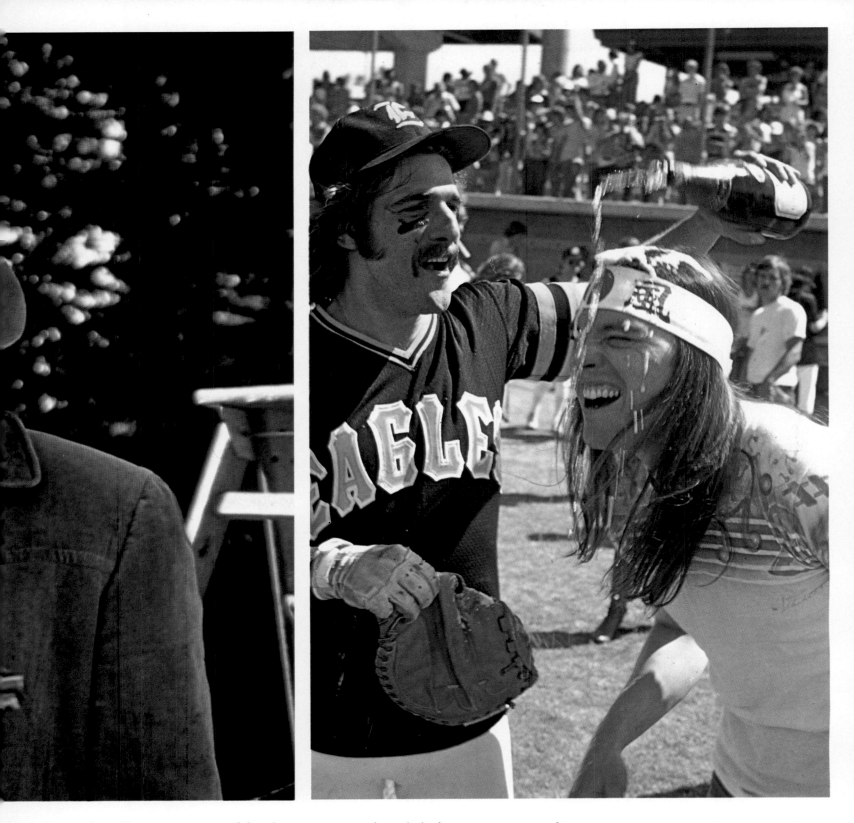

the pop fans. They were successful and now score consistently in the country, pop and easy-listening charts. Dolly even had a disco hit in 1978 with *Baby I'm Burning*. Crossover stars have been helped by the recent interest shown in country music by network TV and movie-makers. Hollywood discovered that films based around country songs, like *Convoy*, and featuring country tunes on the soundtrack like *Every Which Way But Loose* usually did very well at the box office.

Most of the important male crossover artists share a common experience of having had to struggle through many long, hard-working years before finally breaking into the big time as performers. Their strength and perseverance, often in the face of disinterested audiences or unsympathetic record companies, and the depth of their musical experiences, now stand them in good stead and are key factors in their continuing success.

Waylon Jennings and Willie Nelson, the singers most frequently associated with the outlaw movement, have been in the country music business since the Fifties but were not to achieve national fame until the mid-Seventies. They had experienced some success in country music – for Nelson most notably as a songwriter – but both became increasingly disenchanted with the Nashville system and took their musical futures into their own hands. Rejecting the conventional country sound of the Nashville studios in favour of a more rock influenced style they achieved crossover success on a scale probably beyond even their wildest dreams.

above: *For many people country rock means the sound of The Eagles. Here guitarist and singer Glen Frey cools off bass player Tim Schmit after an energetic soft ball game. Country rock developed amongst musicians in the Los Angeles rock scene at the tail end of the Sixties and early bands included Poco, Dillard and Clark and The Flying Burrito Brothers. The Eagles, who formed in the early Seventies, planned their career carefully after watching Poco and the Burritos lose their initial momentum. They made every effort to look, sound, play and write as well as they could. They wanted the respect of their peers, radio play, number one singles and albums, to make great music and lots of money – and they succeeded.*

Charlie Daniels is over forty and has had a long wait for fame. He spent about thirteen years playing low-life bars and honkytonks as a member of The Jaguars before moving to Nashville and making a small fortune as a session man – he has featured on dozens of albums including three by Bob Dylan and Ringo Starr's country album. In 1971 he formed his own band and they have recorded and toured prolifically ever since. The Charlie Daniels Band are the most successful exponents of combining country music with high-energy rock music.

Kenny Rogers, the Texan singer with the relaxed manner, has been making records, on and off, for over twenty years but it was only in 1977 that he became a country superstar following the success of *Lucille*, a worldwide hit. It marked the beginning of his third, and biggest, period of success as a singer.

He first had a recording contract while still at high school in the Fifties and had a hit with a song called *Crazy Feelings* that sold a million nationwide. After university Rogers was in the New Christy Minstrels, then formed The First Edition with whom he enjoyed a second period of fame with a string of hits including *Just Dropped In To See What Condition My Condition Was In, Reuben James* and *Ruby (Don't Take Your Love To Town)* – all of which he still includes in his live act today. The inspired idea to team him with songstress Dottie West has paid high dividends – they now challenge Loretta Lynn and Conway Twitty as country music's hottest duo.

While many of today's male country superstars have had to wait many years for their success the women have tended to be somewhat quicker in making their mark. Dolly Parton, Crystal Gayle and Emmylou Harris, three of the most popular country crossover artists, all had their share of hard work for little pay in the early days but found fame within a few years. Their respective success stories will be chronicled in a later chapter on 'Country Girls'.

above: *Canadian Anne Murray's sophisticated blend of country and pop has been pleasing audiences and winning her awards for over ten years but she's been singing for her own pleasure for much longer. Born in the coal-mining town of Spring Hill, Nova Scotia she says she was singing as soon as talking. In 1963, she auditioned unsuccessfully for the popular Canadian TV show* Singalong Jamboree. *Five years later she tried again, made the show, rapidly became a popular TV star, and before long had a world-wide hit with the song* Snowbird.

opposite: *Linda Ronstadt, the first lady of country rock, was born in Tucson, Arizona into a musical family. She was a member of a popular local folk trio in her teens, then moved to Los Angeles where she helped form The Stone Poneys who recorded four albums for Capitol. Linda went solo in 1971 and made an album with the musicians who later formed The Eagles. A couple of years later she began an association with Asylum Records and producer Peter Asher that led to world-wide fame and fortune.*

As Ronnie Milsap and Kenny Rogers have crossed over into easy-listening pop to find greater success some artists have made a journey in the opposite direction. John Denver, Glen Campbell and Anne Murray are three of the most successful pop singers who have turned to country.

John Denver has crossed many musical barriers in his career. He began playing folk music as a teenager and spent four years in the Chad Mitchell Trio. He seems equally at home whether playing at state fairgrounds, in sophisticated nightclubs or on the set of a TV show. He sings of the American countryside and romance and his best songs have been inspired by life at his home in the beautiful Rocky Mountains in Colorado.

'I'm not a country singer,' explains Glen Campbell when asked, 'I'm a country boy who sings.' He began a long and successful career with Capitol Records in 1967 with a hit called *Gentle On My Mind* and has appeared in movies, including a co-starring role with John Wayne in *True Grit,* and had a popular TV show for several years.

A frequent guest on the show was Anne Murray. She gave up her job as a physical education teacher to become a professional singer and was the first female vocalist from Canada to sell a million records – with a song called *Snowbird.* She dropped her successful girl-next-door image for a more straightforward and sophisticated style. It was a daring move which paid off as she has become an almost permanent fixture on the country and easy-listening radio station playlists and charts.

Rock artists began a flirtation with country music towards the end of the Sixties and a blend of music called 'country rock' had become very popular by the mid-Seventies. Country rock is a hybrid of country, bluegrass and soft rock. The late Gram Parsons can take much of the credit for creating the sound and inspiring others. A talented but tragic figure – he died of heart failure brought on by an excessive consumption of drink and drugs – he had a brief but influential period with The Byrds prior to their *Sweetheart of the Rodeo* album, one of the first country flavoured rock records, and formed The Flying Burrito Brothers who had little commercial success but encouraged dozens of other bands, including The Eagles.

above left: *Crystal Gayle is the younger sister of the long-established country singer Loretta Lynn. Sixteen years younger than Loretta, Crystal was raised in considerably less impoverished circumstances. While still a schoolgirl she travelled with Loretta as a back-up singer under the name of Crystal Bell. Other than an early one-off hit, her career was never properly launched until 1975. Her association with hit producer Allen Reynolds, together with her excellent vocal range, have led to numerous country and crossover pop successes.*

above: *Ronnie Milsap won the CMA Male Vocalist of the Year Award in 1974. He gave up a scholarship to study law at Emory University in order to play with J.J. Cale. He later formed his own band*

playing a mixture of blues, jazz and country but eventually, with the guidance of Jack D. Johnson, began to concentrate on becoming a country star and has had many top five hits including Let My Love Be Your Pillow, *which reached number one in 1977.*

above right: *Singer Kenny Rogers, one of the most consistently successful crossover country superstars of recent years, was born in Houston, Texas, one of eight children. Away from his busy working schedule, Kenny finds time for other pursuits including designing his own house, writing a book, being a keen photographer – his picture of Glen Campbell graces the cover of Glen's* Southern Nights *album – and organizing an annual charity soft ball game in Las Vegas.*

The original four members of The Eagles – formed in 1971 – included members of The Burritos and other early country rock outfits like Poco and Shiloh. Through extensive live work and skilfully crafted albums – including the ever popular *Desperado* – they became the most successful exponents of country rock and between 1972–6 were among the world's top box-office attractions. Country rock had become increasingly unfashionable by the end of the Seventies and few successful bands now play it. Poco, one of the pioneering bands, finally found fame and fortune after ten years when they dropped the country flavouring from their records, and The Eagles themselves, who now tour and record far less prolifically, have moved much closer to rock.

Six months before they formed The Eagles, with fourth member Bernie Leadon, Glen Frey, Don Henley and Randy Meisner were hired by a little known singer called Linda Ronstadt. Their brief association with her was to have a profound influence on her eventual emergence as the most successful female country rocker.

She finds her early recordings with a band called the Stone Poneys – from 1967-9 – embarrassing and the first record she actually liked was *Linda Ronstadt* in 1971 which featured her friends from The Eagles. The record shows a clear country influence and she explains, 'It was beginning to be apparent that country music and rock and roll could be synthesized – people didn't realise that the Everly Brothers and Elvis Presley had been making zillions out of the synthesis for years.' After this album she joined Asylum records with whom The Eagles and other aspiring country rock acts were already signed and, with new producer Peter Asher, improved immeasurably as a recording artist and catapulted to international stardom.

Linda Ronstadt's torchy country rock, Anne Murray's sophisticated country pop, Waylon and Willie's gritty outlaw sound and Kenny Rogers's relaxed balads are very different – few people would probably find them all attractive – but they share common ground both in drawing on strong country music influences and being amongst the most popular and best loved sounds of today.

right: *A log cabin high in the Appalachians. It was in such areas that settlers, highly religious but still making their own brand of whiskey, turned their thoughts about living and dying into the first true country songs.*

THE Anglo-Celts came in the seventeenth century. They settled in the high Appalachians that stretch down through Georgia and Tennessee where, for many years, they lived unaffected by the changes of the outside world.

In an existence that was family-bound and clan-like they clung to an Old World tradition of music, their ballads and dance tunes retaining an easily identifiable Scots-Irish patina. The fiddle was the king of instruments in the mountains. Frowned upon by some as a device of the devil, it was, nevertheless, small and light, easy to tote from place to place. And a solo fiddler was all that was needed to provide the music at a local dance or family get-together. As time passed by, the five-string banjo found its way into mountain music; while the guitar, a descendant of the ancient lute, also became popular, winning more admirers than either the mandolin or the dulcimer, two other instruments that found their way into the string bands of the South-West.

In other areas too, the music of the Anglo–Celts was to be found. For some moved west from Tennessee and Virginia, settling in the Great Plains, meeting other races, creating other sounds – all of which were to become part of country music.

With the advent of radio, the music of the rural musicians became heard over a wide area and won so many new admirers that broadcasting stations throughout the United States began scheduling radio barn dances featuring the folk singers and string bands from country areas. The record companies promptly sat up and took notice. They set up studios in various Southern towns and sent out scouts to locate any performers of talent. However, it was, oddly, in New York that what is believed to be the first true country music record was made. For there, in 1922, a Texan named Eck Robertson and a Virginian called Henry Gilliland strode into the offices of the Victor Record Company (later called RCA–Victor and now known as RCA) and asked if they could record. Fiddle-players both, their appearance – Robertson was clad in a Confederate uniform while Gilliland wore cowboy attire – bemused the people at Victor, who eventually did record the duo, though few sales resulted.

Recordings by Henry Whitter, Fiddlin' John Carson and several other old-time musicians followed – but it was not until 1925 and the advent of a recording session involving Al Hopkins and his string band that the music received the nomenclature by which it was to be known for many years. The band had just recorded six titles under the supervision of Victor talent scout Ralph Peer, when the latter suggested that Hopkins should think of a commercial name for his then unchristened outfit. Hopkins is said to have thought briefly and then said: 'Call the band anything you want – we're nothing but a bunch of hillbillies from North Carolina and Virginia, anyway.' So the band became The Hillbillies and shortly, what had been known variously as old-time music, and hill music, became catalogued as hillbilly – staying that way until the Forties when, following pressure on the record companies by various artists who resented being labelled as country hicks, the terms 'country' or 'country and western' came into general use.

It was Ralph Peer who also gained the credit for discovering Jimmie Rodgers and The Carter Family, two of the most important names in country music history. Rodgers, during his brief life span, became the biggest selling star in country music,

THEY CALLED IT HILLBILLY

above: *A small-time bluegrass get-together. During the Sixties, a new and youthful audience found the music to its liking, with the result that bluegrass musicians found themselves frequently employed not only on country shows but also on huge folk and rock bills. In 1977, a tribute to Earl Scruggs, perhaps the greatest banjo-player of all time, was filmed and recorded. Among those taking part were The Byrds, Joan Baez, The Dirt Band, Doc and Merle Watson, David Bromberg and Tracy Nelson.*

opposite: *Jim and Jesse McReynolds from Coeburn, Virginia. With their band, The Virginia Boys, they have brought bluegrass music to virtually every corner of the world. Creators of a highly individual vocal harmony style, Jesse is also noted for possessing a unique style of mandolin playing. The grandsons of an old-time fiddler who recorded for Victor, the McReynolds brothers made their radio début in 1947 and became regulars on the Opry in 1964.*

while the Carters, Alvin Pleasant (A.P.) Delaney Carter, his wife Sara and his sister-in-law Maybelle Addington Carter, popularised such songs as *The Wabash Cannonball, Wildwood Flower, Keep On The Sunnyside, Lonesome Valley, I Shall Not Be Moved* and A.P.'s own *I'm Thinking Tonight Of My Blue Eyes.* Though the group split up in 1943, nearly seventeen years after their first recording session, and though A.P. died in 1960, Maybelle continued to be an important influence on the Nashville scene – sometimes appearing on the *Johnny Cash Show* – right up till 1978, when she too died. But her daughters, who include June Carter Cash, still help to keep the Carter tradition alive.

Today, the term 'country music' has almost replaced the 'country and western' identity tag by which the music was known to some during recent years. The name sprang from the glut of cowboy songs that accompanied many Hollywood westerns during the Thirties and Forties. At that time, no low-budget sagebrush saga seemed complete without its share of western songs (often penned by city writers who thought of country music as strictly cornball fare) rendered by such heroes as Gene Autrey, Ken Maynard, Dick Foran, Jimmy Wakely, Eddie Dean, Tex Ritter and Roy Rogers, most of whom were singers first and cowboys last. Autry, who provided the top country record every year from 1932 through to 1936 and who still figured amid the top sellers in 1945, started out on Tulsa radio in 1928, while Ritter was a law-student who made it onto the Broadway stage before co-hosting a radio barn dance and cutting his first records in 1934. Roy Rogers had a musical background too, being Leonard Slye, an ex-peach picker and truck driver who worked with such outfits as The Rocky Mountaineers, The Hollywood Hillbillies and The International Cowboys before forming The Sons of The Pioneers and spending some considerable portion of time sitting around camp-fires on the Republic Pictures sets.

Later, the singing cowboy was to ride into the sunset virtually forever, though scores of major westerns were to be prefaced by songs of the saddle, often rendered in ultra-dramatic manner by such pop stars as Frankie Laine. However, the services of some country singers were retained for such purposes and Tex Ritter's *High Noon* theme remains a classic of the genre, while Roger Miller's *Waterhole Three* ditty

Gene **AUTRY** *and* **CHAMPION** *Jr.* *Wonder Horse of the West*

Robin Hood of

proved that not all western themes need necessarily be of the type guyed in Mel Brooks's *Blazing Saddles* spoof.

To many, the instrumental sound of country music has always seemed dominated by the tear-stained cry of the pedal-steel guitar and the dobro, both variants of the Hawaiian guitar. Polynesian music became extremely popular in the United States during the early twentieth century and the Hawaiian guitar, which was laid flat in the lap and played with a steel bar which was slid along the strings, can be heard on many historic recordings, including some made by Vernon Dalhart and Jimmie Rodgers. The dobro, which is basically a guitar with raised strings and a metal resonator, was originally devised by John, Ed and Randy Dopyera in 1925, obtaining its name from the first two letters of Dopyera and the first three of Brothers. Along with its chief rival, the national steel guitar (which had three resonators), the dobro made a tremendous impact upon the sound of country music during the Thirties and Forties. The acceptance of the pedal-steel guitar (an instrument which has the facility of bending

above: *A publicity still from one of Gene Autry's many Republic pictures. An easygoing Texan, he was one of the best known movie stars in the world during the late Thirties. Raised on a cattle ranch, Gene became a railroad telegrapher, later using one of his free passes to head for New York where he recorded for a multitude of labels, eventually achieving a half-million seller with* That Silver Haired Daddy Of Mine. *Orville Gene Autry appeared in over 100 films and, to many, was the singing cowboy. Only his horse, Champion, had as many fans.*

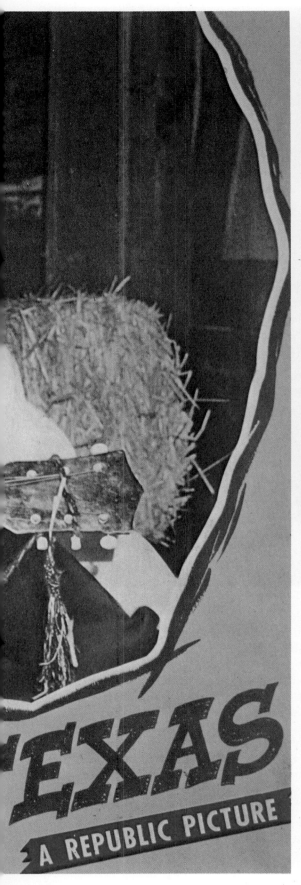

above right: *Two revered bluegrass figures – Bill Monroe and Mac Wiseman. If any man can claim to have invented bluegrass it's Monroe, who formed his Bluegrass Boys in 1938 and joined the Opry a year later. During his early career, he went out with a roadshow that usually comprised a gospel quartet, a comedian, a fiddle-player, a couple of additional singers and a dancer who did buck and wing. Mac Wiseman is just one of the many fine musicians who have served an apprenticeship with Monroe; others include Don Reno, Flatt and Scruggs, Jimmy Martin, Vassar Clements, and the ill-fated Stringbean.*

notes) dates from 1954 when Bud Isaacs played a pedal-steel solo on *Slowly*, a Webb Pierce single which became one of the major country hits of that year.

The national and the dobro were both attempts at obtaining a bigger sound from a guitar – but it was electrical amplification, which came about during the mid-Thirties, that revolutionised country music and helped it compete against the powerhouse bands of the swing era. Not that country musicians didn't form swing bands. They did. But often, where such as Artie Shaw, Benny Goodman and the popular swing kings would feature a saxophone section or a trio of trumpets, their country counterparts would frequently feature a brace of fiddles or a steel guitar playing the same riffs, though horns were far from unknown with the 'western swing' bands, as they became known. These bands, led by men like Milton Brown, Spade Cooley, Bob Wills and his brother Johnnie Lee Wills, swung with much the same impact as those of Glenn Miller and the Dorseys. And if their waltzes weren't quite so sophisticated, they often became a lot sprightlier – for though the city jazzmen generally hated playing $\frac{3}{4}$ tempo dance music, the country musicians, with their barn dance heritage, treated such twirl-arounds as *Mexicali Rose* and *The Waltz You Saved For Me* with more affection. During the Forties such affection paid off handsomely for Pee Wee King, leader of The Golden West Cowboys, when his *Tennessee Waltz* became a huge selling record for Cowboy Copas, creating such an interest among pop artists that in 1950 no less than eight versions of the song – by Patti Page, Jo Stafford, The Fontane Sisters, Spike Jones, Guy Lombardo, Les Paul and Mary Ford, Anita O'Day and Rosemary Clooney – found a place in the pop Top 30.

While western swing had, and still has, its share of devotees, others hailed the merits of bluegrass music. Derived from the music of the traditional string bands, bluegrass was popularised by Bill Monroe and His Blue Grass Boys during the late Forties and early Fifties. Usually banjo-propelled, with such instruments as the mandolin, guitar, bass and fiddle in tow, the music has become so accepted by a wide audience that hardly a rural car-chase or wayward truck scene seems to appear on either the cinema or TV screen without the benefit of some Flatt and Scruggs-type bluegrass accompaniment, the best example of this being in the 1967 movie *Bonnie and Clyde*, during which the duo provided *Foggy Mountain Breakdown* – virtually the national anthem of bluegrass – with telling effect.

Five years later, in 1972, bluegrass was to win further friends among movie buffs when Eric Weissberg and Steve Mandell's *Duellin' Banjos* was featured in *Deliverance*, a starring vehicle for Burt Reynolds and Jon Voight.

Country-gospel too has grown in popularity. Many major artists include a gospel

above: *A shot of The Oak Ridge Boys taken shortly after the time of their* Old Fashioned, Down Home, Hand Clappin', Foot Stompin', Southern Style Gospel Quartet Music *album, the last album of purely sacred material to be recorded by the group before they opted for a more secular approach. For years one of country's most popular gospel outfits – vying with The Blackwood Brothers and The Statesmen in crowd-pulling power – The Oaks walked away with the Dove Awards of 1972, when they were not only acclaimed as Best Group but also won the Best Album, Best Instrumentalist and even Best Album Cover sections. Formed in Oak Ridge, Tennessee in 1957 by Smitty Gatlin, the group has appeared on numerous record labels over the years – Cadence, Checker, Starday, Skylite, Heartwarming, Warner Brothers, Columbia, ABC and MCA – providing the last two companies with the sort of pop-country hits that have even found favour among rock-addicts.*

medley as a regular part of their act, while trying to calculate the number of shows that terminate in hand-clappin', all-join-in versions of Hank Williams's *I Saw The Light* or The Carters' *Will The Circle Be Unbroken?* would probably keep a highly sophisticated computer in full-time employment!

There is a strong heritage of religion within country music that harks back to the camp-fire meetings of the early settlers. Often they farmed in remote areas where the only hope on hand was of the spiritual kind. Accordingly, the prayers and hymns offered were rendered with considerable warmth and fervour and this feeling still pervades the gospel side of country today. But then, there are two distinct sides of country gospel, one being represented by the gospel quartets and sacred song singers of the Gospel Music Association, the other by various artists who have chosen to blend the sacred with the secular in order to spread the word to a wider and perhaps more needy public. Some, like The Oak Ridge Boys, have actually crossed the dividing line and have left their church hall dates behind them, becoming reviled for so doing. Equally, there have been those such as Wanda Jackson and Connie Smith, who have headed in the opposite direction, quitting the commercial side of country music in order to devote their time to purely religious activities. And some have managed to straddle both sides of the fence with apparent ease, a case in point being that of Jimmie Davis, composer of *You Are My Sunshine* and twice Governor of Louisiana, who not only became a member of the Country Music Hall of Fame but also won numerous awards for his work in religion – including an award as the Best Male Sacred Singer of 1957. Not that being involved in religious matters has always meant turning one's back on one's bank manager. When Tennessee Ernie Ford cut his *Hymns* album for Capitol Records in 1956, he not only demonstrated to his *16 Tons* fans that Jesus was worth singing about, he also provided the company with a disc that was to remain in the US charts for 276 weeks, selling well over two million copies in the process.

Sometimes the Lord moves in financially rewarding ways!

Perhaps the least familiar country music sound is that of the cajun variety. Cajun music, a mixture of blues, country and French traditional songs, originated among the Arcadians (hence cajun), the original French settlers of Arcadia (now Nova Scotia), who were deported by the British in the eighteenth century. Perhaps as many black

and creole musicians as white now play and sing cajun music, though a white accordionist named Joseph Falcon is generally credited with making the first cajun record in 1928. However, the music remained a minority interest until 1946 when Harry Choates, a young writer who was also a prodigious drinker, had a hit record with his *Jole Blon*. Jailed at the age of 28 for wife and child desertion, Choates died within a few days of his arrest – but his *Jole Blon* lived on and inspired scores of other musicians, including Doug and Rusty Kershaw and Jimmy C. Newman. Least known of the country sounds it may be – though as long as there's someone to sing Hank Williams's *Jambalaya*, with its references to crawfish pie and filet gumbo, the cajun music is unlikely to be entirely forgotten. One thing that has never been forgotten in country music is humour. The Opry developed a tradition for comedy-instru-mentalists right from the very onset. Uncle Dave Macon, with his banjo and supply of clean jokes, set the pattern in the early days and from then on such folk as Whitey Ford ('The Duke Of Paducah'), Lonzo and Oscar, Cousin Emmy and Homer and Jethro carried on the tradition of jokin' and pickin'. Cornball their humour may well have been – but many were superb musicians, Jethro Burns (the Jethro of Homer and Jethro) proving to be not only a fine country instrumentalist but also just about the finest jazz mandolinist in the world. Singers too have often wanted to try their hand at the comedy side of country, often creating an alter ego in order to do so. Ferlin Husky did so with great success, appearing as Simon Crum, hick philosopher supreme, while Sheb Wooley, of *Purple People Eater* (and *Rawhide* TV series) fame, became Ben Colder, providing such comedy records as *Harper Valley PTA – Later That Same Day* and *Almost Persuaded No. 2*. And though in recent years Archie Campbell, the high-kicking Grandpa Jones and the chunky Junior Samples have vied with the other funsters on TV s *Hee Haw* to provide the corniest jokes of the year, country comedy's mainman is currently Jerry Clower, a one-time sales director who became so successful with his hilarious sales talks that he later became a full-time entertainer and the creator of several enthusiastically received comedy albums.

Laughs and tears. Country music has them both in abundance, somewhere in there among the western swing, the country-pop, the gospel and traditional, the bluegrass and the cajun. Those who claim that it's samey just haven't taken the trouble to really listen.

above: *Maybelle, June and Anita Carter indulging in some acappella work on* The Johnny Cash Show. *Mother Maybelle, who died in 1978, was the last surviving member of the original Carter Family, who recorded on Victor's historic recording session held in Bristol, Tennessee, during the summer of 1927. Together, the Carters – A.P. a singer with a fine bass voice, Sara, his auto-harp-playing wife, and Maybelle, his guitar-picking sister-in-law – created whole new standards in country music, recording over 300 songs. Many have become time-honoured favourites all over the world. The Carters pioneered several unique instrumental sounds, Maybelle's distinctive guitar-playing being much imitated. Maybelle's daughters, June, Anita and Helen, first began working with the group during the late Thirties, at a time when the Carters were broadcasting over the powerful X stations (so named because of their call letters) that operated just over the border in Mexico. But later the family was to split, Maybelle working with her daughters, and A.P. and Sara forming their own family group.*

right: *The Grand Ole Opry is unique – a truly remarkable institution that has presented authentic country music live every Saturday night for over fifty years to millions of radio listeners over WSM's 50,000 watt clear channel. The show has never missed a broadcast.*

NASHVILLE, Tennessee is the country music capital of the world. Every important record company dealing in country music has offices here: there are over forty recording studios and ten times that number of music publishing houses. The Tennessee capital is also known both as 'The Athens of the South' and 'The Wall Street of the South'. The Athens title comes from its importance as an educational centre – there are fourteen colleges – and its Greek Revival architecture including an actual, full-sized replica of the Parthenon of Athens in Centennial Park. Nashville's reputation as a financial centre derives from the considerable insurance and banking interests in the town.

Nashville lies close to the Appalachian Mountains, where country music has many of its roots, but it is initially due to an insurance company's sponsorship of the music that the town has become 'Music City USA'. WSM, a Nashville radio station owned by the National Life and Accident Insurance Company, thought a weekly barn dance programme would be an excellent way of selling insurance policies to families in rural America.

In 1928 George D. Hay, the self-styled 'Solemn Old Judge', stood in front of a microphone and announced the first *WSM Barn Dance* with a ninety-year-old fiddler called Uncle Jimmy Thompson who claimed to be able to 'fiddle the bugs off a 'tater vine'. From such humble beginnings grew the show that became known as *The Grand Ole Opry* which is now synonymous with country music and Nashville.

Before long, hillbilly musicians everywhere wanted to perform on the *Opry*, even if they didn't get paid, and listeners across the USA – WSM broadcast over a clear channel that could be heard in several states and even parts of Canada – saved their hard-earned money for a trip to Nashville to see the show.

Public demand for tickets meant it had to transfer from the radio station to a number of different locations, that included an old tabernacle and the War Memorial Building, before settling into a permanent home at the Ryman Auditorium, in downtown Nashville, in 1941.

Early favourites included performers with names like Dr Humphrey Bate and his Possum Hunters and the Dixie Clodhoppers, and the first artist to achieve national fame through the programme was Uncle Dave Macon. Instrumental music, mainly banjo and fiddle dominated, was the mainstay in the early years and any singing was incidental. All this changed in the late Thirties with the arrival of the Opry's first singing star Roy Acuff and his band of Smokey Mountain Boys. His success opened the way for more singers like Cowboy Copas, Ernest Tubb and Eddy Arnold.

Roy Acuff found country music a lucrative business and, with a pop songwriter called Fred Rose, invested money in Nashville's first publishing company. The establishment of Acuff–Rose in 1943 paved the way for the opening of recording studios, record company offices and the other prerequisites of the music business. Within fifteen years Nashville really was the country music capital.

In the Forties and Fifties the Opry boomed, growing side by side with the emerging music industry. It was the leading radio barn dance and was instrumental in launching the careers of Hank Williams, Marty Robbins, Bill Monroe, Charlie and Ira Louvin, Lefty Frizzell and many more.

NASHVILLE AND THE GRAND OLE OPRY

above: *Unknown singers and guitar pickers played at Tootsie's in the hope that someone important might take a liking to them. The owner Tootsie Bess was a good friend to stars and struggling musicians alike, but had a notorious habit of ejecting customers who became too rowdy with the aid of her long hat pin. Tootsie's is still popular with tourists who come to stare at the memento-lined walls. But the club owner has gone, she died in 1978 after a long battle with cancer.*

George Hay, who had played a vital part in the development of the Opry by persuading well-known performers to appear and discovering fresh talent, didn't like the advent of the singing stars – who inevitably forced out many of the bands who had been popular in the Thirties – and his involvement with the show became less and less important. His role was reduced to that of host and spokesperson until the early Fifties when he became ill and had to leave the show.

The success of the Grand Ole Opry inspired other radio barn dances – most notably the Louisiana Hayride which attempted to emulate its Nashville-based rival but ended up being a talent pool for the show. When an act had established itself on the Hayride it usually moved on to Tennessee. This happened with such stars of the future as Jim Reeves, Hank Williams, Faron Young and the Wilburn Brothers, and further ensured that Nashville was the capital of country music activity.

In the mid-Fifties rock 'n' roll arrived on the scene, killing most of the radio barn dances, ending several careers and forcing the country music industry to change in order to survive. The new sound, developed in the early Sixties by producers like Billy Sherrill and Chet Atkins, became known as 'countrypolitan' or the 'Nashville Sound'. It was smooth, often orchestrated, and opened the music to a larger, more urban, audience.

The Opry, which only survived the rock 'n' roll era with difficulty, didn't change so dramatically, retaining its traditional approach. This pleased the hard-core country fans but meant the Saturday night radio show was no longer reflecting the current country music scene.

The Opry today is still grand, even if many of the big names no longer appear, but it

isn't so old, because the show is now housed in a plush modern building at Opryland, a vast entertainment park, nine miles out of town – ideal for family outings. After experiencing a series of shows and rides with musical themes – like the 'Wabash Cannonball' a terrifying roller coaster – you arrive at Opry Plaza and the new 4,400 capacity theatre, opened by Richard Nixon in 1974, which has comfortable seats and air conditioning that are a far cry from the conditions of its old home.

The Ryman Auditorium was built as a church by a riverboat captain named Thomas Ryman who had experienced an astonishing conversion after a lifetime of drinking and gambling, but served its religious purpose for a mere seven years before becoming a home for first classical music concerts and then the Opry. The uncomfortable wooden church pews remained to the end and, although the place had a wonderful atmosphere, the discomfort suffered by artists and fans alike eventually forced the move to Opryland.

Nashville visitors today can still visit the Ryman in the Broadway area of downtown. The former centre of country music is increasingly run down and tourists have to pick their way past 'adult' bookstores and striptease clubs as they check out Ernest Tubb's famous record store, Loretta Lynn's Western Store and Tootsie's Orchid Lounge. For years aspiring country singers came to Tootsie's, a small beer joint, in the hope of being discovered by one of the country music stars who patronised the place between performances at the nearby Opry.

While the tourists are visiting Broadway and Opryland the aspiring singers and songwriters of today are haunting the offices on 'Music Row' – 16th and 17th Avenues and their connecting streets – the area that is the centre of the Nashville music industry.

above: *The Ryman Auditorium in downtown Nashville was the Opry's home from 1941 to 1974. When it closed RCA records purchased the famous stage backdrop which featured an advertisement for W.E. Stephens, a clothing concern that had sponsored the show since 1929. Later, the record company had the backdrop cut into thousands of pieces which were given away as souvenirs to buyers of* Stars of The Grand Ole Opry, *an album that contained tracks by Uncle Dave Macon, Pee Wee King, Minnie Peal, Del Wood, Bill Monroe and many other stars who had performed in front of the Stephens advertisement.*

above left and right: *The $100,000 customised car and the guitar-shaped swimming-pool are just two of the assets possessed by Fifties superstar Webb Pierce. Born in Louisiana, Pierce first gained a spot on local radio before breaking through on Shreveport's* Louisiana Hayride *show. The possessor of a fine band during the early Fifties – his sidemen included Faron Young, Floyd Cramer and Jimmy Day – Webb soon began gathering various plaudits, netting the American Juke Box Operators' Number One Singer Award in 1953.*

As he became less successful in the charts, he turned more to the business side

This centre is tightly knit in contrast with the other two important music cities New York and Los Angeles.

It is not easy being an aspiring songwriter or singer in Nashville. The competition is incredible and the odds against being discovered, even if you have real talent, are huge. John Sebastian wrote a song in the Sixties called *Nashville Cats* that mentioned the town's 1,352 guitar pickers – and he wasn't far wrong. A small number have regular employment as highly paid session men and they jealously guard their privileged status, but most are earning a living as best they can, taking jobs as waiters, cleaners, etc., between poorly paid musical jobs.

Songwriter Don Schlitz is a good example of a hopeful songwriter coming to Nashville – except that he was one of the very few that broke through. Arriving from North Carolina on a Greyhound bus in 1973 he had nothing except two suitcases, a battered guitar, fifty dollars and a dream of becoming a successful singer/songwriter. For five years he worked nights at the university as a computer operator and by day pitched songs at anyone who showed an interest, played in some of the local bars and hung out with other musicians.

Then, one day, a song he had written called *The Gambler* was picked up and several people recorded it, Kenny Rogers eventually taking it to the top of the country pop charts. Every singer who has made it in Nashville will attest to the fact that there is no quick way to the top – you have to pay your dues on the street before getting the opportunity to break into the big time, and most people, sadly, never get that chance.

The Nashville that Don Schiltz broke into in 1979 was going through something of an

identity crisis – not apparent to the fans still convinced that this was an exclusively country music town – but obvious to the people down on music row. There was increasing concern and confusion about the way Nashville's music was heading – the question in everyone's head was 'to be country or not to be country'?

In the Sixties things were more straightforward. The bosses of big record companies were happy for their Nashville chiefs to do as they wished, to record who and what they liked in their own styles. People such as Chet Atkins and Billy Sherrill were able to wield remarkable power at their respective operations at RCA and CBS. Then country music became very big business – artists like Dolly Parton were gaining widespread popularity and going to Los Angeles for new management, the outlaws went over the heads of their Nashville chiefs to renegotiate their contracts, and records began selling in millions rather than the hundreds of thousands that country chart toppers usually sold – so the bosses in New York and on the West Coast began having far more to do with the music.

Country music was being recorded in London, Los Angeles and New York – Nashville lost its monopoly though not its popularity as a recording centre. The reputation of Nashville's session men encouraged non-country performers to record there and today the amount of rock, pop and even soul recorded in Music City is greater than ever. Some of the younger music executives have taken the word 'country' off their cards and now talk about making Nashville music. But country remains the mainstay of the studios and although the musical future of the town is going to become increasingly diversified, Nashville will remain the country capital.

of country music, purchasing interests in radio stations, a record company and a publishing company, the last named proving extremely lucrative. However, Webb still cuts records from time to time and always finds a ready audience any time he chooses to reprise past hits like In The Jailhouse Now, I Don't Care *and* Love, Love, Love. *Some of his old discs are also much sought after by rockabilly fans, who still rave about his* Teenage Boogie *and keep Webb in high regard.*

The swimming pool shown here lies directly across the road from the Country Music Hall of Fame and can be visited by the public. The remarkable car is also on display.

right: *Boxcar Willie adopted his hobo guise after spending many years trying for a spot on the Grand Ole Opry garbed as a rhinestone cowboy. And though his guise is purely a gimmick, his railroad songs – punctuated with uncannily accurate loco whistle sounds – are rendered with disarming sincerity and affection.*

COUNTRY'S had a love affair with trains since way back when. The wreck on the Cleveland and Ohio, in 1890, is still remembered in songs such as *Engine 143*, while the death of railroad engineer Casey Jones, in a disaster that took place in 1900, is hardly likely to be forgotten as long as there are pickers in Nashville.

An object of hatred to the Indians, who saw the railroad as a steel ribbon which was to choke the life out of their society, the train represented the hopes of tomorrow and the dreams of yesterday to the settlers of the West. From a train could step a loved one from the old home town. From a train could tumble enough supplies to keep a man alive when the fight against nature seemed all but lost. A train could make anything happen. And so the railroad engineer became a hero, and his locomotive a valiant iron horse, to be revered and held in high esteem.

By 1916, 254,000 miles of track criss-crossed the United States, the station had become the focal point of many a town and there seemed to be hardly a homestead that was out of earshot of the mournful train whistle. At the same time, the revolutionary sound of the phonograph was beginning to reach the public. Henry Whitter, a millhand from Virginia, was probably the first country musician to record a railroad song. He learnt *The Wreck Of The Southern Old '97* from a fellow mill worker in 1914 and, some nine years later, Whitter, who played guitar, fiddle, piano, harmonica and organ, could be found heading for New York to record the number for Okeh Records. The record was released in January, 1924, and was heard by a light opera singer named Marion Try Slaughter, who recorded under a multitude of aliases. As Vernon Dalhart, he waxed versions of the song twice during 1924, once for Edison and again for Victor, the second version selling over one million copies and establishing Dalhart as a seminal figure in country music history. Following the success of *The Old '97*, other songs of the railroad were committed to shellac with some alacrity. Soon, record catalogues reported the availability of such discs as *The Baggage Coach Ahead*, *The Lightning Express*, *John Henry* and many others that utilised a railroad theme. The stage was set for the arrival of Jimmie Rodgers, 'The Singing Brakeman', a railroad man who was to become country music's first true star.

The son of a section foreman on the Modile and Ohio line, Jimmie had become a water-carrier at the age of 14, learning blues and railroad songs from the black workmen he supplied. For 14 years he worked on lines throughout the south-west, usually as a flagman or breakman. However, he was not a healthy man and eventually, a victim of tuberculosis, he gave up the rigours of railroad life to try his luck as an entertainer. Rodgers found it a precarious occupation initially, experiencing many set-backs. But after recording for Victor in 1927, Rodgers became an overnight sensation, much of his material, such as *Ben Dewberry's Final Run*, *Train Whistle Blues*, *Brakeman's Blues*, *Waiting For A Train* and *Hobo Bill's Last Ride* reflecting his former way of life. His records sold in millions but his success was destined for but a brief ride down the track. On 26 May 1933 Rodgers died, after just five years at the top. The provider of many fine train songs, he became one of the first musicians to be elected to Nashville's Country Music Hall Of Fame. Now hailed as 'The Father Of Country Music', his plaque reads: 'Jimmie Rodgers (September 8, 1897–May 26, 1933).

RAILROAD BLUES AND TRUCKSTOP DUES

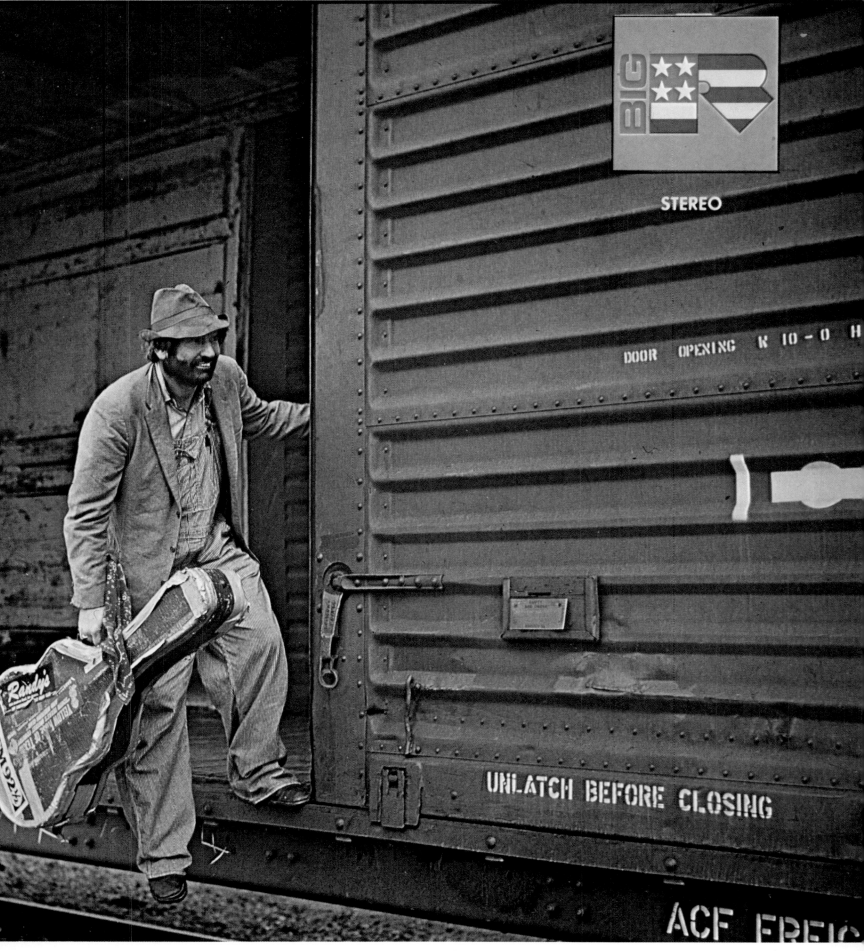

above: *The much-loved Jimmie Rodgers –
'The Singing Brakeman'. He worked on the
railroad for nearly fourteen years before
moving on to become the first true country
music Superstar. He was also the star of the
first country music film, appearing in a
1929 short entitled* The Singing Brakeman
*in which, attired as a brakeman, he sat in a
railroad depot cafe and sang* Waiting For
The Train. *Rodgers was elected to the
Country Music Hall of Fame in 1961, nearly
forty years after his death.*

'The Singing Brakeman' . . . Jimmie Rodgers's name stands foremost in the country
music field as 'the man who started it all'. His songs told the great stories of the singing
rails, the powerful steam locomotives and the wonderful railroad people that he loved
so well. Though small in stature, he was a giant among men, starting a trend in the
musical taste of millions. Rodgers's body was returned from New York to his
hometown of Meridian, Mississippi, by a train that pulled in, late one night, blowing
long and low on its mournful whistle. It was, perhaps, the most apt requiem any
musician ever had.

Since Rodgers's death, the love affair has continued. During the Thirties, Roy Acuff
hitched a musical ride aboard *The Wabash Cannonball* – a song so famous that a train
was named after it! – following this with excursions on *The Streamlined Cannonball*,
The Fireball Mail and the *Night Train To Memphis*, while in more recent times, Johnny
Cash has headed for success with *Orange Blossom Special*, Roger Miller has chugged
gainfully along on *Engine, Engine No. 9* and Elvis Presley has set the *Mystery Train*
a'rockin' on down the tracks.

Cash, perhaps more than any other singer since Rodgers, has embraced the
romance of the railroads, recording a concept album, *Ride This Train*, that took the
listener on a musical hobo ride across America, while Merle Haggard, who is reputed
to own one of the largest collections of model trains in the world, produced *My Love*

Affair With Trains in 1976, a marvellous album that paid tribute to the railroads and the days when steam was king.

But while such remembrances of smoke-breathing monsters still remain dear to the hearts of some country songwriters, the sons of Casey Jones seem to have lost a little of their glamour in these days of diesels and Amtrak. Today it's the trucker, rather than the railroad man, who has become the hero of the transport saga. He is depicted as a tough, kindly, and seemingly never-sleeping speed king, willing to conquer unclimbable mountain roads, cross breaking-point bridges and fight armies of hi-jackers in his whole-hearted effort to win through. Equipped with his CB radio he has become James Bond on 16 wheels – but with a touch of Will Rogers that makes him homespun and human. Country music caught on to this new breed of supermen during the late Thirties, when Cliff Bruner and Moon Mullican recorded Ted Daffan's *Truck Driver Blues*, though perhaps the most successful trucking anthems have emanated from the likes of Dave Dudley, whose *Six Days On The Road* in 1963 is reputed to have commenced the current truck song cycle; Red Simpson, whose *I'm A Truck* was a top country disc in 71; and Red Sovine, provider of *Phantom 309*, the all-time trucking ghost story, plus *Teddy Bear*, a saccharine-sweet tale of a crippled child and some heart-of-gold truckers that won Red a gold disc at the age of 58. *Teddy Bear* also served to emphasize the camaraderie achieved by drivers by means of their CB

above: A scene from Smokey And The Bandit, *a box-office smash which combined spectacular chase scenes with country music by Bill Justis and Jerry Reed, the latter also having a leading role in the film. Trucking films can, perhaps, be traced to* The Wages of Fear, *a French film released in 1953. Television, too, has for many years been sold on the trucking theme.* Cannonball, *a Canadian series, ran for 39 episodes during the late Fifties and* Movin' On *lasted for 48 episodes from 1974–5. Country music has greatly benefited – bluegrass and Nashville travellin' music often being used as a background to the action.*

radios – though this aspect of trucking was utilised to even greater effect by William Fries, who wcn an award for a TV advertising campaign he mounted on behalf of the Mezt Bread Company. Creating a fictional Old Home Bread trucker named C.W. McCall, he used his own voice on the commercials, gaining so much acclaim that Fries/McCall became a recording star, lining up such hits as *The Old Home Filler-Up And Keep On A Truckin' Café*, *Wolf Creek Pass* and *Black Bear Road*. Then, in 1976, he released *Convoy*, a classic single that not only made the world aware of the CB code and McCall's 'Rubberduck' call sign but also sparked off a movie starring Kris Kristofferson, Ali MacGraw and Ernest Borgnine and featuring songs by Merle Haggard, Billie Jo Spears, Doc Watson, Glen Campbell, Crystal Gayle and many others.

But though the kings of the road would appear to be the current glory riders, the railroad legends of Jimmie Rodgers live on in the hearts and voices of such men as Haggard, Hank Snow and country music's oldest new star, Lecil 'Boxcar Willie' Martin, an entertainer who sometimes seems to be half singer, half locomotive.

Meanwhile, back at the Opry, *Orange Blossom Special* and *Wabash Cannonball* are still wheeled out with almost monotonous regularity. And so the love affair still moves on down the line . . .

above: Kris Kristofferson starred in Convoy, *an all-action movie directed by Sam Peckinpah. It was filled with country music by Gene Watson, Billie Jo Spears, Billy 'Crash' Craddock, Crystal Gayle, Merle Haggard and many others – and sparked off the trucking films genre.*

opposite: Taking it easy is Dave Dudley whose trucking song Six Days on the Road *provided him with a major hit in 1963. Since then he has had a flow of chart hits has included such asphalt-flavoured titles as* Truck Drivin' Son of a Gun, Trucker's Prayer, Keep on Truckin' *and* Rollin' Rig – *all of which have endeared him to the Nashville local of the Truckers' Union, who presented Dudley with a solid gold security card as a token of their esteem.*

right: *Ernest Tubb's original record shop on Nashville's Broadway, just around the corner from the Ryman Auditorium. The shop was opened in 1947, the same year that Tubb commenced his* Midnight Jamboree *shows on radio station WSM. Later, live segments of the programme began being broadcast from the shop itself.*

TO many, Roy Acuff *is* Nashville. An Opry star for many years, he was nominated as State Governor in 1943, 1945 and again in 1948, winning the primaries on the last occasion and capturing just about the largest slice of the vote ever achieved by a Republican candidate in what has always been considered an impregnable Democrat stronghold. And when in 1974 the new Nashville Opryhouse was opened, it was Acuff who met President Nixon and proceeded to give him yo-yo lessons – much to the delight of the attendant media. The possessor of a mournful, mountain vocal style, Acuff became an all-American favourite during the war years, even edging out the then teen-dream Frank Sinatra on some important polls. Indeed, legend has it that when the Japanese attacked at Okinawa, they yelled, 'To hell with Roosevelt, to hell with Babe Ruth, to hell with Roy Acuff,' as they charged forward.

While Acuff is a native Tennessean, Ernest Tubb, another member of the Country Music Hall of Fame, was born in Texas. Always regarded with affection in Nashville, the genial Tubb, who today is as active as ever, has lent a hand to many a career. It was he who arranged Hank Williams's first appearance on the Opry, while Hank Snow, Johnny Cash, Cal Smith and Jack Greene are among those who readily admit their debt to the Texas Troubadour. When, in 1978, Tubb decided to record a solo album for his own 1st Generation label, half of Nashville volunteered to join in on the sessions, Conway Twitty, Loretta Lynn, Merle Haggard, Willie Nelson, Waylon Jennings, Charlie Rich, Marty Robbins, Johnny Cash, Johnny Paycheck, George Jones and Cal Smith all dropping by Pete Drake's studio where the album was being pieced together. But then, he has always worked in good company, even gaining a couple of hits by recording with the Andrews Sisters in the late Forties. Bing Crosby, who at one time worked for the same label as Tubb, paid him the compliment of recording Ernest's self-penned *Walkin' The Floor Over You* – but it was Tubb's own recording that really made the grade, becoming a million-seller in 1942. The song has become a country standard and can still be heard today, often on the *Midnight Jamboree*, one of country music's most famous live radio shows, a programme which has been broadcast from Tubb's Nashville Record Store since 1947, the show being currently transmitted from the Texan's new shop in Demonbreun Street.

It was Tubb, too, who was responsible for *The Soldier's Last Letter*, another World War II hit. But undoubtedly the country entertainer who really cashed in on the country's patriotic mood was yodeller Elton Britt, a prolific recording artist – he recording 672 singles and 50 albums for RCA alone – who made a record called *There's A Star Spangled Banner Waving Somewhere* – a song about a cripple who yearned to fight for America – and was subsequently awarded the first gold disc ever presented to a country artist.

The war years did much to advance the popularity of country music. To many US servicemen fighting in Europe, Africa or the Pacific, the sound of Tubb, Acuff and Britt was the real sound of home. The radio request shows were often deluged with letters asking for an airing of the latest Gene Autrey single, Al Dexter's *Pistol Packin' Mama* or Red Foley's flagwaving *Smoke On The Water*. The American Federation of Musicians helped too – by going on strike!

GOLDEN AGE HEROES

The AFM had asked that the recording companies set up a fund for musicians left unemployed by the growth of the record industry – jukeboxes had replaced bands in many clubs, while radio stations increasingly used discs instead of live musicians – and when the companies refused to donate to such a scheme, the musicians refused to make any more records. But the minor labels, many of which specialized in what was then termed 'hillbilly' music quickly settled with the AFM and proceeded to promote their wares, while such giants as Columbia and Victor continued to face the recording ban for over two years. But they did not fail to notice that country music had captured a large audience during the interim – and Decca's first release after coming to terms with the musicians was a cover version of *Pistol Packin' Mama*, recorded by Bing Crosby and The Andrews Sisters.

RCA-Victor learnt too. They signed Eddy Arnold.

Many country historians tend to ignore Arnold's part in country music, classifying him as a crooner, someone roughly akin to Crosby, Sinatra or Perry Como. And while it's true that Eddy's voice was smooth and totally commercial, an attribute which enabled him to play guest spots on virtually every leading radio show, Arnold had been born in Tennessee and worked his way around the country circuit as vocalist with Pee Wee King and his Golden West Cowboys. As country as they come, he became dubbed the 'Tennessee Ploughboy'. Though he didn't record until shortly before the end of the war, by 1947 Victor were able to announce that they had sold nearly two and three-quarter millions of Arnold's discs in that year alone. Then in 1948 came *Bouquet Of Roses*, *Anytime* and *Just A Little Lovin' Will Go A Long Long Way*, all million-sellers, and from then on, Arnold seemed to have fans queuing at the record shop any time his label scheduled a release. Sales did eventually taper off in the early Seventies, at which time he parted company with RCA and moved to MGM. However, by 1976 he was back with his old label once more and riding high in the charts with *Cowboy*, perhaps one of his finest singles. No one can fault Eddy Arnold on durability!

The American Dream – the farm boy who becomes a star despite all adversity – is a familiar story in country music history. Not all such tales have happy endings though. Few could be more tragic than that of Spade Cooley, the one-time Hollywood extra who leased the Santa Monica Ballroom in 1946 and used the venue as a base from which to launch what was numerically the biggest band in country music and proved very successful on record, radio and early TV. He later was jailed for murdering his wife and, though he was released after a lengthy sentence, he died soon after gaining his

opposite: Bow balancing is just one of Roy Claxton Acuff's on-stage gimmicks. However, he is not only a showman but also a fine musician and a singer with a highly individual style. Though injured in a 1965 road accident, he was soon back on the road again – even making trips to entertain servicemen at the Vietnamese front. In 1979, at the age of 76, Roy was still making records and planning headline appearances at concerts.

above: 'Howdy! I'm just so proud to be here!' Minnie Pearl, who's been making Opry audiences laugh since 1940, is seen gaining a guffaw from Roy Acuff, a fellow entrepreneur in the fast food business. Born Sarah Ophelia Colley, she hails from Canterville, Tennessee – though she's been plain Minnie from Grinders Switch for as long as anyone can remember, her straw hat and old-fashioned dress becoming part of country music tradition. The price tag on the hat is another part of that same tradition, the story being that during her first Opry appearance she rushed onstage, unprepared, and forgot to remove the tag, which she now retains as a good luck charm.

left: *Jim Reeves's big opportunity arose when Hank Williams failed to appear on a* Louisiana Hayride *show and Jim was asked to stand in for him. His performance impressed the boss of Abbott Records so much that Reeves was signed and recorded 'Mexican Joe', a number one country hit in 1953.*

top: *Slim Whitman's Fifties recordings of* Indian Love Call, Rose Marie *and* Secret Love *each sold over one million copies. Slim, who claims that his biggest musical influences were Jimmie Rodgers and Wilf Carter, first arrived in Nashville in 1949 and today he still registers a reasonable number of US country hits – but it's in Europe where the 'sold out' signs go up.*

above: *During the late Forties and early Fifties Eddy Arnold's recordings of* It's My Sin *and* Bouquet of Roses *were slotted in alongside Bing Crosby and Stan Kenton on the request shows and his appeal was such that he was hardly out of the country music top ten for a period of twenty-two years.*

freedom, playing a benefit concert in California.

If Cooley's death passed comparatively unnoticed in music circles, the loss of Jim Reeves in a 1964 air crash gained the kind of attention normally afforded a national disaster. A Texan, weaned on the sound of Jimmie Rodgers, Reeves, like Eddy Arnold, possessed the kind of voice that appealed to a pop audience as much as a country one. Though a great favourite in the States during the Fifties, signing to the Opry in 1955, thanks to the inevitable friendly nudge from Ernest Tubb, it was not until 1960 and his version of Joe and Audrey Allison's *He'll Have To Go* that Reeves crossed the Atlantic and captured the imagination of the British public. From then on it was sheer adulation all the way, his records filling chart positions for months on end – the news of his death accelerating sales to such an extent that the British *New Musical Express* Top 20 Album Chart of 12 September 1964 contained no less than nine Reeves recordings. Even today, Reeves retains a massive fan following in Britain, and there are fans who admit to viewing *Kimberley Jim*, his only film, over a hundred times. To maintain such unusual British interest, RCA, with the co-operation of Mary Reeves, Jim's widow, have continued to reissue and reprocess Jim's old recordings using technical devices of such ingenuity that in 1977, thirteen years after his death, they were able to create the illusion that the Texan was singing a duet with himself by feeding one of his tapes through a studio gadget which altered the tone and pitch of Reeves's vocal and then added the resulting harmony line to the original recording. The sleeve notes on Jim Reeves's album never indicate that he has in fact died. And seemingly, as far as many are concerned, he hasn't.

Slim Whitman is another US country singer whose courtship of the British pop public has resulted in a long-lasting relationship. In his homeland, Slim – though he hasn't notched up an American pop single hit since 1957 – is considered a reasonably successful country artist. But in Britain he is almost a superstar, playing sell-out tours every time that he appears, his albums often reaching the coveted number one spot in the charts. In 1977, he sang and yodelled so effectively on his British-produced *Red River Valley* album that it outstripped every rock album in its climb to the top. Now 56, he attracts new fans on every tour he makes, while his original admirers still turn up by the drove and squeal for *Rose Marie* and *Indian Love Call*, the Rudolf Friml operetta favourites that Slim yodelled into chart status back in the early Fifties. Says Whitman, 'I still get people bring up their programmes from the Palladium, 1956. Okay, I signed that programme in 1956; I signed the same programme in '57. I also signed the same programme in 1970, 1973 or whatever. Which proves you've got the same people plus the people that have come in because of radio and TV advertising. And it's a new generation of kids too that have come in. They've never heard of *Rose Marie* before. They say, "Hey! that's a great song." To them it's a new song.'

A song of the Twenties, sung by a star of the Fifties to the youth of the Eighties. Sometimes the flag of country music waves quite oddly.

right: *Johnny Cash at San Quentin. He once played a concert at the penitentiary at a time when Merle Haggard was a leading light in the prison band.*

ASK Bobby Bare to comment on the theory that he and Tom T. Hall are the only two real storytellers in Nashville and he's likely to say, 'Yeah, that's probably true. We're very close friends anyway – but the problem is that when we get together Tom wants to drink brandy. And after three shots I just get drunk. But he always talks me into it by saying, ''It's only fruit juice, Bobby Joe.'' Man, that fruit juice just wipes me out quick – I find that I'm soon talking to myself!'

The craggy-faced Bare has always been something of a Nashville rebel, without being bracketed as an outlaw. He made his first hit record out on the West Coast using then unknown sessionmen such as Leon Russell, Jimmy Seals, Dash Crofts and James Burton. When he headed for Nashville in the early Sixties he made a specific request to RCA's Chet Atkins that none of the usual Music City session stars be used on his recordings. 'I was so new that I felt intimidated by them,' he admits. So a number of up and comers were employed – 'new musicians . . . guys like Charlie McCoy and Boots Randolph.' It seems that Bare was always ahead of the crowd. Today he has changed little. He still does things that makes 'em scratch their heads in Nashville. His recent *Sleeper Wherever I Fall* album, which once more found him using a considerable number of fresh faces, cost over a hundred thousand dollars, an enormous amount for a country album. 'That's nothing though if you're thinking in terms of a million-seller,' reckons Bare. 'Record companies make a lot of money off albums and they could get around seven million dollars back.'

Sleeper was recorded for CBS, the company which at the close of '79 had such singers as Johnny Cash, Marty Robbins, Johnny Rodriguez, Johnny Paycheck, Moe Bandy, George Jones and Willie Nelson on its roster. Cash is perhaps the most charismatic of them all. He has been with the company ever since 1958 when he left Sam Phillips's Sun label, after a run of hits that included *I Walk The Line*, *Guess Things Happen That Way* and *Ballad Of A Teenage Queen*, songs which made him a hero with the rock 'n' rollers.

Dressed in black, the possessor of a face that suggests it was designed by some wayward sandblasting machine, Cash looks every inch a heavy. The way he totes a guitar like a machine-gun, his appearances at Folsom Prison and San Quentin, his portrayal of an ageing gunfighter in the movie *A Gunfight* – all have added to the legend that Cash is a hard man, a hell-raiser who has spent more than his fair share of time in the penitentiary. In fact he is very much a family man who has many of his relatives on his touring show, records a goodly proportion of gospel songs and once made a film about a visit to the Holy Land. It's true that he did pop pills for six or seven years of his life, while he tried to keep up the pace that fame had set for him. However, the theory that he is a jailbird has little substance, Cash's prison record comprising just one day and one night behind bars – the latter stay following an arrest for picking flowers at two a.m.! Later he wrote a song about the incident:

> Well, I left my motel room down at the Starkville motel.
> The town had gone to sleep and I was feeling fairly well.
> I strolled along the sidewalk, 'neath the sweet magnolia trees,
> I was whistling, picking flowers, swayin' in the Southern breeze.

TODAY'S MAINSTREAM MEN

I found myself surrounded, one policeman said, 'That's him – come along
wild flower child, don't you know that it's two a.m.?'
They're bound to get you, 'cause they got a curfew,
And you go to the Starkville city jail.

So John R. Cash is not really as tough as many think. But he has got a great, grainy,
will-he-or-won't-he-make-it hunk of a voice with more character than most. Which is
why he sells a lot of records.

Certainly, Merle Haggard's background is more violent. Even as a teenager he
became involved in armed robbery, also logging charges of car theft and fraud before
finally spending two years in San Quentin for attempted burglary. As a candidate for
an all-American hero, he would appear to have stood little chance. But he became one
in 1970 when he wrote *Okie From Muskogee,* in which he expressed such sentiments
as:

We don't smoke marijuana in Muskogee
We don't make our trips on LSD.
We don't burn our draft cards down on Main Street.
We like living right and being free.

Soon the song became an anthem for the silent majority. Even the President wrote and
congratulated Haggard for his clean-living and patriotic view of life. The good guys, it
seems, don't always wear white.

The young Chicano Johnny Rodriguez might easily have headed the same way as the
teenage Haggard but for the intervention of Joaquin Jackson, a Texas Ranger with a
sense of social responsibility. Then known as Juan Rual Davis Rodriguez, Johnny
initially fell foul of the law when he and some friends stole and barbecued a couple of
goats. Later he found himself in jail for a more minor offence and probably would have
made a return visit had not Jackson found him a job singing at Brackettville's Alamo
Village resort, where he was heard by Bobby Bare and Tom T. Hall, who advised him –

above: *Marty Robbins is one of the most popular singers in country music, his long string of number one hits including* Singing The Blues, A White Sport Coat, The Story Of My Life, El Paso, Don't Worry, Devil Woman *and* My Woman, My Woman, My Wife. *When he returned to the Opry after major heart surgery in 1970, the fans' delight was such that they wouldn't let him leave the stage.*

left: *Though George Hamilton IV is regarded as country music's international ambassador and has netted his own TV series in Canada and Britain, his last major US hit was with* Abilene *in 1963.*

opposite top: *Despite his success with* Okie From Muskogee, *Merle Haggard was actually born and bred in California, his birth taking place in a converted boxcar in Bakersfield, where his parents had made their home after leaving the dustbowl of East Oklahoma.*

opposite bottom: *The quiet man of country – Don Williams, CMA Vocalist of The Year in 1978.*

above: *The Statler Brothers – who took their collective name from a box of tissues they espied in a hotel room – hail from Virginia and were once known as The Kingsmen. Their first hit was a big one, Statler Lew De Witt penning* Flowers On The Wall, *which leapt out of the country listings in 1965 and quickly climbed the pop charts, eventually claiming a top five position and winning the Brothers a couple of Grammy Awards. Since then they've hardly stopped collecting various plaudits, time and time again being judged Top Vocal Group at the annual CMA Award ceremony.*

opposite: *One of the few black singers to make any impact on country music, Charley Pride – seen here accepting a special award from British RCA – came from a thirteen-strong family that sharecropped a cotton farm on the Mississippi Delta. At the age of fourteen he bought a mail order guitar for ten dollars and set out to become the next Hank Williams or Roy Acuff – two of Pride's boyhood heroes. But it was as a baseball player that he initially shone, making the Memphis Red Sox team in 1954. Luckily for the world of country he was later unable to make headway in sport, at which point he began devoting his energies to a musical career achieving a high percentage of home runs for his record label.*

presumably between tots of brandy – to head for Nashville and ultimate fame.

If Rodriguez was the first Chicano to make a breakthrough in country music, then Charley Pride was the first black musician really to make the grade in Nashville. An odd state of affairs in retrospect, when one remembers that the very first musician to play on the Opry was DeFord Bailey, a black harmonica player. Whatever the reasons – and despite the massive success of Ray Charles's country albums – black was not considered beautiful in country circles for many years, even Bailey ending up in charge of a shoe-shine stand. Pride's management predictably decided to play things safe at first. When his initial single was released by RCA, no photographs or biographical information were provided for the benefit of the media. He sounded white and right and so his songs were played on radio stations that might have ditched his record into the nearest waste-paper basket had they known the colour of Charley's skin. Luckily for Pride, the ruse worked and helped establish him as a genuine country artist. By 1971 he had gained the Entertainer Of The Year crown from the CMA though this success did little to open up the flood-gates to black artists. A handful, such as Linda Martell, Stoney Edwards and O.B. McClinton have made some impact along the way. Overall, though, nothing has changed.

Though white, Ronnie Milsap originally sounded very black indeed. So black in fact, that he found himself frequently playing on bills alongside acts like The Miracles and Bobby Bland. Not that Milsap has ever thought or cared much about colour – for he was born blind. He originally idolised Ray Charles and sang songs like *Let's Go Get Stoned* in a manner so like Ray's that his bar-room listeners must have thought they were hearing things. As time moved on, he softened down and switched to country music, signing a management deal with Jack D. Johnson, the very man who had master-minded Charley Pride's career. He has since proved to everyone's satisfaction that he's a fine pianist, a show-stopping impressionist and a vocalist who can switch from country ballad to raunchy rock with consummate ease. Six years after Pride, Milsap also grabbed the Entertainer Of The Year accolade. Never was an award so richly deserved.

Every Nashville biography has its twist. Sometimes it seems that Music City is just full of characters living lives originally planned by a manic Hollywood script writer. Freddie Hart is a case in point. He ran away from home when he was seven, joined the Marines at 14 and subsequently spent the next few years fighting against the Japanese in such places as Iwo Jima, Okinawa and Guam. Today, he is not only a tremendously successful singer, having recorded *Easy Living*, winner of the CMA Best Song award

above: *Freddie Hart was helped on his climb up the country music ladder by the legendary Lefty Frizzel, who bought his first stage outfit and took him on the road. Freddie joined Frizzel on Columbia at the end of the Fifties before moving on to Kapp, supplying each of these labels with a steady stream of hits. But it was with Capitol in '71 that he made the final breakthrough, his recording of* Easy Loving *proving the first of six consecutive number one hits.*

in both 1971 and 72, but is also the possessor of a black belt in karate. Not that Hart is aggressive. In fact, he is an extremely likeable, kindly man who would rather spend his time promoting the school he runs for handicapped children. Sometimes he seems to perhaps be searching for his own lost childhood. One way or another he makes a lot of friends for country music and is a credit to Nashville.

So too is the quietly spoken Moe Bandy, who spent a portion of his life as a bronco buster, busting almost as many bones as he did broncos while he learned his trade. Nowadays, he is simply the best bar-room singer on the scene, his songs bearing such beer-stained titles as *Here I Am Drunk Again*, *The Bottle's Holdin' Me* and *All My Beer And All My Friends Are Gone*. Actually, he usually looks pretty sober and is so baby-faced that in '79 he decided to grow a beard in order to adhere more closely to his sawdust floor image.

above: *Though Bobby Bare's name first hit the headlines through his chart recording of* Shame On Me *in 1962, he'd previously enjoyed a massive pop hit with his* All American Boy, *which had climbed to the number two spot in the US charts four years earlier. Unfortunately, the disc was wrongly attributed to Bill Parsons – with the result that Bare, who had sold the song rights for a mere $50 and then joined the army, remained a nobody for a few extra years. But his success with* Shame On Me, *was followed by hits with* Detroit City *and* 500 Miles Away From Home, *resulting in immediate elevation to pop idol status and a role in* A Distant Trumpet, *the Hollywood western.*

left: *Moe Bandy before he opted for a beard – 'Because my face looked kinda fat!' One of six children weaned on the records of Jimmie Rodgers – his grandfather owned an extensive collection – Moe also spent much of his childhood listening to The Mission City Playboys, a band organized by his dad*

IN rural America in the Twenties and Thirties women traditionally occupied a subordinate role to men and this is noticeable in country music's early years where women, though frequently found in groups and acting as accompanists, were very rarely to be found as performers in their own right. The solo female singers that we take for granted today were an almost unknown species until the Forties and Fifties; indeed until the Sixties there was never more than a handful of very popular female country singers.

Nevertheless music was as much a part of women's lives as men's fifty years ago, and they played important roles in the development of country and appear on pioneering recording sessions and radio shows. Alongside A.P. Carter in The Carter Family were Sara and Maybelle, two girls from Virginia, who had married A.P. and his brother Ezra. The Carters – 'The First Family of Country Music' – were recorded in August 1927 at the historic sessions organized by Ralph Peer that also marked Jimmie Rodgers's recording début. The very first Grand Ole Opry featured Uncle Jimmy Thompson accompanied by his niece Mrs Eva Thompson on piano, and several of the early Opry bands had female members, such as Theron Hale and Daughters.

It was not until the late Thirties that a girl experienced national success as a country performer. Patsy Montana, long associated with the Prairie Ramblers with whom she sang on the *National Barn Dance* radio show, became the first woman to sell a million copies of a country record with *I Want To Be A Cowboy's Sweetheart* in 1938.

Her success served as a precedent and an inspiration for others who enjoyed popularity in the Forties. These included Rosalie Allen, a country yodeller known as the 'Prairie Star', who was especially popular in the north-east of the USA; Martha Carson, a talented singer and songwriter whose fame spread with regular appearances on radio shows and at state fairs with her husband James Carson; and Molly O'Day, a very special singer who quit recording and performing before her prime and never achieved the role, as the first great female singer in country, that many felt she deserved.

Country music's first consistently successful female singers were Rose Maddox and the incomparable Kitty Wells. Alabama born Rose began her career as lead vocalist in a band with her four brothers. The Maddox Brothers and Rose were the most popular family outfit of the post-war years establishing their reputation on *The Louisiana Hayride* before going on to Opry performances and making hit records. Rose went solo in the latter half of the Fifties and made frequent appearances on the country charts both as a solo performer and as part of a duo with Buck Owens.

Between 1952 and 1965 Kitty Wells was the undisputed 'Queen of Country Music' – no other woman was as consistently popular and successful in the country charts. Though born in Nashville, Kitty had to travel thousands of miles around America before she finally found fame there on the stage of the Opry. She had married Johnny Wright of the Johnny and Jack stage act in 1938 and toured with them as a singer – Johnny being responsible for her name change from Muriel Deason after the folk song *Sweet Kitty Wells*.

They toured extensively during the war years and in 1947 Kitty won a guest spot on the Opry and became a regular on *The Louisiana Hayride*. Her popularity on the radio

COUNTRY GIRLS

top: *Loretta Lynn has an enormous following. A consistent producer of hits since 1962, she was the first female artist to win the CMA's Entertainer of the Year in 1972; and in 1976, her autobiography,* Coal Miner's Daughter, *was in the* New York Times *best-selling book list for nine weeks.*

opposite: *Olivia Newton John exploded on to the American music scene in 1974 with a British-produced song* Let Me Be There *which was a major success in the country charts. Olivia's knowledge of country music was minimal at the time, but she went on to win the CMA Female Singer award – beating Dolly Parton and Loretta Lynn – which led to the formation of the Association of Country Entertainers who insisted that Olivia was not a country singer. Attitudes have since changed and Olivia can take much of the credit for making it easier for pop singers to be accepted in country music circles.*

show led to a record contract with Decca in 1952 and the first release was a massive hit record *It Wasn't God Who Made Honky Tonk Angels* and marked the beginning of her long reign as Country Music Queen. Because there had been no charts in the Thirties, when Patsy Montana had her million seller, Kitty became the first woman to top the country charts. She repeated her success over twenty times in the next thirteen years.

The Sixties saw a proliferation of female country talent. Patsy Cline probably came closest to taking Kitty Wells's crown at the beginning of the decade with several huge hits including *Crazy* and *I Go To Pieces* but her career was tragically cut short in 1963 when she was killed in an air crash. Her record company continued to issue her songs and she had hits for several more years. Other popular country girls in the Sixties included Wanda Jackson, a child prodigy who had worked with Hank Thompson's western swing outfit before discovering rock 'n' roll and touring with the young Elvis. She returned to country music in 1961 and had several hits during the next ten years. Like Connie Smith, another popular star of the Sixties, Wanda has strong religious convictions and now makes only gospel records.

Skeeter Davis had been a member of the successful Davis Sisters in the Fifties, a duo whose career ended after a horrible car accident that left Betty Jack Davis dead and Skeeter badly hurt. After several months of mourning she returned to recording and performing and in 1955 began a career as a solo country singer. She was very popular in the Sixties scoring her biggest hit with *The End of the World* in 1962. During the same period Melba Montgomery found fame as half of a duo with George Jones – from

top: Tammy Wynette first turned to country music to supplement her income after her marriage broke up, leaving her with three children to support. Her most successful song, Stand by Your Man, *was a huge hit in America and Britain, and sold a record number of copies. She was the CMA Female Vocalist Of The Year in 1968, 1969 and 1970.*

far left: Dolly Parton first started recording *at the age of thirteen. In 1970 Joshua reached number one, and she has had many other top five hits. In 1975 and again in 1976 she won the CMA Female Singer of the Year Award. Apart from her success as a country singer and entertainer, she is also a gifted songwriter, much of her work being inspired by her early life. In recent years she has also begun to make an impact in films and on television.*

left: *Texas born singer Billie Jo Spears is internationally popular especially in England where numerous tours and TV appearances have established her as a firm favourite with both pop and country fans alike. She made her first record when she was thirteen, had a couple of small hits in 1968–69, though it wasn't until 1975 and the success of* Blanket On The Ground *that her reputation as a major talent was established.*

1962 to 1967 – an association that yielded several hit records including the country classic *We Must Have Been Out Of Our Minds*. Something of a specialist at duets – she worked with Gene Pitney and Charlie Louvin amongst others – she has also had considerable success as a solo singer.

Jean Shepard, widow of Hawkshaw Hawkins who was killed in the same horrifying air crash, as Patsy Cline began her career in the Fifties but scored her greatest success in the Sixties though retaining a distinctive Fifties style for her music. She was especially popular with country fans concerned about the inroads pop was making and she continues to be a vigorous campaigner to 'keep country pure'.

Three of the new girl stars of the Sixties were to find fame in the Seventies on a scale that had previously not been witnessed in country music. Loretta Lynn, Tammy Wynette and Dolly Parton all began life in humble surroundings but have risen to become amongst America's most popular and best loved entertainers.

Tammy Wynette has earned the title 'The First Lady of Country Music' after nearly fifteen hit-filled years in which she has become the most honoured performer in the business. Her successful musical career has sadly been parallelled by a private life that has given her more than a fair share of heartache. There have been five marriages, including a stormy seven-year association with the singer George Jones, and she has suffered burglaries, arson attempts on her property and a horrible kidnapping, that have left deep emotional scars. Most of Tammy Wynette's songs are about sadness in love, of loneliness, longing and loss, which have given her the reputation as 'the sad-eyed lady with the sob in her voice'. During her early years in Nashville, she met up with Billy Sherrill who instantly saw her potential and launched her career with a name change – 'You look like a Tammy to me'. Sherrill had remarkable success finding the right sound and songs for Tammy's emotive voice. The 1966 release *Apartment No. 9* was to be the first of many hits that were the epitome of the commercial Nashville sound. Tammy is suprisingly modest about her voice and her success: 'People say I have a unique sound, but I don't hear it. I believe, like Billy Sherrill, that the song is more important than the singer and I've been lucky in getting the material to record.'

Bright, bubbling and bouncy – Dolly Parton is larger than life, the kind of character who could have stepped out of a fairy story. Born the fourth child of a family of twelve in a desperately poor, inbred community at Locust Ridge in Tennessee's Smokey Mountains, she loved fairy tales as a child and imagined she could be Cinderella.

Dolly developed her childlike, playful, though never childish image from an early start and began singing on the radio when she was only ten. Strong and self controlled she was clearly determined that her dreams of fame and riches would come true. In Nashville she worked with Porter Wagoner on his TV show and records, developed her solo career as a country singer then joined a Los Angeles based management company and dropped her country band in favour of a slicker, more pop-orientated group. Country music traditionalists were horrified by the new image, but most of her fans stayed loyal. As she explained in an interview with the *New York Times*, 'I don't want to leave the country but to take the country with me wherever I go. I am Dolly Parton from the mountains, that's what I'll remain'.

Loretta Lynn began life as the daughter of a very poor coal miner in Butcher's Hollow, Kentucky, married when she was barely fourteen and became the teenage leader of a country band. A song called *Honky Tonk Girl*, released on a local label, became a small hit and attracted the attention of people in Nashville. She had four daughters by this time but with a husband happy to support the family she moved to Music City and trekked around the record companies, finally securing a contract with Decca – before long she had made the country charts.

Since 1962 she has enjoyed an almost unbroken run of country hits both solo and as half of a duo with Conway Twitty. With her husband Oliver 'Mooney' Lynn she has established a number of highly successful music-related business interests including the Loretta Lynn Rodeo Company and a chain of Western Wear stores. She is now one of the richest women in country music and her remarkable rags to riches story is best told by Loretta herself in the autobiography *Coal Miner's Daughter* which was a runaway bestseller and has now been filmed.

Dolly, Loretta and Tammy have been at the top of the country music tree for several years but are now being challenged by a number of younger singers including Crystal Gayle, Barbara Mandrell and Emmylou Harris. Brenda Gail Webb, Loretta's little sister, is best known as Crystal Gayle. Though sisters, they inhabit different worlds – Crystal is married to a Greek law student and when she is at home, as Mrs Vassilios Gatzimos, has a private life totally separated from music. Loretta, on the other hand, seems to spend every waking moment involved with some aspect of the music business.

Crystal began singing with her sister and her first recording contract had been arranged by Loretta but after a few years she wisely decided to pursue an entirely separate career and become established in her own right. She came under the wing of one of Nashville's best new producers of the Seventies, Allen Reynolds, who used the highly commercial sound for her that had worked so well with Don Williams. In 1977 she

left: *Tanya Tucker in explosive mood – a promotional shot, taken in 1978, to publicise Tanya's rock-orientated* T'n'T *album.*

above: *The same Miss Tucker, the way she was in her Nashville teenage queen era. A hit-maker at thirteen, Tanya later caused a minor uproar with her recording of* Would You Lay With Me In A Field Of Stone?, *a song which expressed sentiments rather frowned upon by the more straight-laced elements of Music City. But Tanya was actually kept on a tight rein. When she came to London on her sixteenth birthday, her mother came too!*

top: *Once a coffee house folk singer, Emmylou Harris teamed up with Gram Parsons during the early Seventies and moved into the world of contemporary country music. Her Hot Band has always featured some of the finest musicians on the country-rock circuit.*

beat Dolly Parton, Emmylou Harris and her own sister for the coveted CMA Female Singer of the Year award.

Barbara Mandrell won the same award in 1979. She is a talented singer equally at home with country, R&B, rock and pop tunes, an accomplished musician (she was proficient as steel guitar, bass, banjo, and saxophone by the time she had reached her teens) and an efficient business woman. Her considerable self-confidence and musical experience from playing in her father's band The Mandrells stood her in good stead when she moved to Nashville in 1968 and began a solo career.

Her popularity grew through the Seventies and was given a considerable boost when she began a musical association with producer Tom Collins in 1975. She works astonishingly hard somehow managing to look after her young family (who travel on the road with her), lead a softball team and run numerous business interests.

Emmylou Harris can take much of the credit for introducing real country music to young rock fans. While Linda Ronstadt and other West Coast artists have been playing country diluted with soft rock she has featured material that is considerably more authentic. She first came to prominence as the singer with Gram Parsons on his two country rock albums *GP* and *Grievous Angel*. After his death in 1973 she considered offers from a number of different record companies before signing with Warner Brothers who wisely reunited her with the musicians who had worked with Gram. They were amongst the best and highest paid session men in the business and included Glen D. Hardin and James Burton who had been in Elvis Presley's band. Known as The Hot Band, their support on record and in concert was important in getting her solo career off to a strong start.

Emmylou has had considerable success with revivals of classic country songs by artists like The Louvin Brothers and has maintained her popularity with young rock audiences. As country singers move towards pop for greater success it is good to see someone who began in country rock selling more records as she returns closer to her country roots.

It is too early to tell who will be the most successful country stars of the Eighties but it's a fair bet that several will be girls who achieved their first hits in the Seventies. Potential superstars of the future could include Janie Fricke, once a session singer, who is moving from singing on the background of other people's records to making her own hits; Debby Boone, the daughter of Fifties pop star Pat Boone, she had a major pop and country hit with *You Light Up My Life*; Susie Allanson an attractive singer in the Linda Ronstadt mould; Tanya Tucker the teenage sensation of the early Seventies who has yet to achieve the widespread crossover success that is predicted for her; and Dottsy the songstress from Texas who has been performing in public since she was only twelve.

right: *The rodeo dust that sold a trillion Lone Star beers! Often the male patrons of Texan dance-halls attempt their terpsichorean chores with one hand clutching their favourite girl and one hand gripping their favourite canned brew. But they sure are appreciative of good music!*

TEXAS leads the USA in oil production, cattle raising and cotton growing. It is also the state with the richest musical heritage. Country, blues, rock 'n' roll, conjunto (the music of Texans of Mexican descent) and western swing – at the very roots of modern rock music – have certain of their origins deep in Texas.

There are two main reasons for the rich mixture of musical styles in Texas. Firstly, the state became home to a diverse number of ethnic cultures – Southern white, Negro, German, Cajun (from the neighbouring state of Louisiana) and Mexican, and if the people themselves didn't mix a great deal their music did, forming a melting pot of styles. Secondly, the geographical position of Texas makes it both part of the South – sharing the same country music traditions of states like Tennessee and Georgia – and also the West – sharing the cowboy influence. It was in Texas that country and western first met.

The Lone Star state has provided country music with some of its greatest and most influential musicians and writers. Cowboy singing stars Gene Autrey and Tex Ritter were born there as were George Jones and 'Gentleman' Jim Reeves. Jimmie Rodgers, the 'Father Of Country Music', made eastern Texas his base – an early hit was *T For Texas* – while Ernest Tubb 'The Texas Troubadour', Lefty Frizell and Ray Price earned their musical apprenticeships in the infamous honky tonks and bars of their home state.

Many of today's brightest and best country talents draw strength from the musical roots of Texas. Willie Nelson and Waylon Jennings returned there for inspiration, after rejecting the mainstream Nashville sound which they believed was restricting their work, while outsiders like David Alan Coe, Jerry Jeff Walker and Asleep At The Wheel love the music and the place so much they have adopted Texas as their home state. Many up and coming young talents like Guy Clark, Townes Van Zandt, Rodney Crowell and Joe Ely are all Texans.

Austin is the capital of Texas – a surprisingly small city for so large a state. Willie Nelson moved there from Nashville at the beginning of the Seventies and became, if not the creator, at least the catalyst for the new progressive country or outlaw music that was to bridge the gap between the tastes of long-haired hippies and the middle-aged, working-class rednecks. Some of the over-excitable music press began to give the impression that country music was about to move its headquarters from Tennessee to Texas. Nothing, of course, could have been further from the truth because Austin, though boasting a plethora of good clubs and musicians, did not have even the most basic requirements for recording and releasing records.

Texas was important for its musical heritage to the new breed of country musicians of whom Nelson and Jennings were the leaders. The basic, earthy simplicity of country music, which had somehow been lost in the creation of the Nashville sound, was still prevalent in Texas. Additionally there was a healthy disregard for convention – Texan musicians have never been noted for their conformity to set styles and patterns and they cheerfully cross musical barriers to add a new flavour or sound.

Today, perhaps the best loved Texan musician from the past is Bob Wills. He was a bandleader who experienced enormous popularity in the South-West in the late Thirties and during the war years with western swing – a hybrid style including blues,

DEEP IN THE HEART OF TEXAS

country, and swing jazz. His band, with popular singer Tommy Duncan and brilliant guitarist Eldon Shamblin, arrived for gigs in a bus with the head of a longhorn steer on the front. Their music was all but forgotten in the Sixties but young musicians in the Seventies led a revival of interest.

Wills was born on a ranch near the tiny town of Turkey, Texas – where they still hold an annual festival in his honour – and began playing the fiddle when he was ten. He worked with Milton Brown, a pioneering western swing musician, in the Aladdin Laddies in Fort Worth. The band became the Light Crust Doughboys when they were employed by a flour company to promote their product over a daily radio show. Wills left in 1933 after a disagreement and set up his own band in Oklahoma. Starting as a twelve piece, Bob Wills and his Texas Playboys grew in time to an eighteen-piece orchestra with fiddles and horns to the fore.

San Antonio Rose became their best known song – their recording sold a million, as did Bing Crosby's cover version, which was popular in the northern USA where Wills was little known. At his peak Wills was said to be paying more tax than any other American entertainer.

Though western swing went out of fashion in the Fifties Wills continued to tour until he was forced to stop by ill health in 1962. A revival of interest in his music began in the early Seventies inspired most notably by the enthusiasm of young bands, like Asleep At The Wheel and Alvin Crow and His Pleasant Valley Boys, and Merle Haggard. In December 1973 Wills, the surviving members of his Original Playboys and Haggard got together to make some new recordings. Sadly Wills suffered a stroke midway through the session and never regained consciousness, though he didn't die until 1975. Several members of his band have since reformed, under the direction of Leon McAuliffe, and play concerts and have issued new records on Capitol – they include fiddler Johnny Gimble, pianist Al Stricklin and vocalist Leon Rausch.

Bob Wills Is Still The King recorded by Waylon Jennings is the best known musical tribute to the man. Jennings, a central character in the outlaw movement, is a doggedly independent singer who appeals to a remarkably wide range of the public, generating enthusiastic responses at concerts from hard core country fans, rock audiences and the sophisticated regulars at showcase clubs in New York and Los Angeles.

He had become a successful mainstream singer by the early Seventies but decided

above left: *David Allan Coe's life story story sounds like a synopsis for a country song – abandoned by his parents when he was nine, twenty years in prison including an (alleged) spell on Death Row for the murder of an inmate, five or six wives and then fame as a country singer. Coe arrived in Nashville in 1967 decked out in the eye-catching guise of the Mysterious Rhinestone Cowboy. He won a recording contract quickly but had to wait several years before success as a songwriter and singer.*

he wanted more control over his music and, following the example of Willie Nelson, tried to re-negotiate his contract. The RCA bosses in New York agreed, giving him unprecedented creative control over choice of material – which meant he could use the songs of his friends like Billy Joe Shaver – and have his own band, The Waylors, playing for the first time on his records.

Few people imagined that Waylon, now well into his thirties, could become a star with his gypsy-like image and a combination of old fashioned, raw-edged country and rock. But he did, probably beyond even his wildest dreams. *Wanted – The Outlaws*, a compilation album featuring songs by Jennings, his wife Jessi Colter, Willie Nelson and Tompall Glaser, sold in unheard-of proportions for a country record and launched him into the superstar category. Since then all his albums have gone gold and his singles, solo efforts or duets with Willie, Johnny Cash or Jessi, have been chart

above: Willie Nelson, one of the biggest stars of contemporary country music, was born in humble surroundings near Waco, Texas. He finished what little formal education he had by the time he was twelve and had a variety of jobs in the music business in honky tonks and radio stations. His life in the roughest parts of Texas gave him plenty of inspiration for songs and he wrote prolifically. Though acknowledged as a fine songwriter since the Fifties he had to wait until 1975 before he was recognized as a performer.

above: *Music critics have been unanimous in praising Joe Ely from Lubbock as one of the finest new talents to emerge from the Lone Star State in years, but radio station programmers and record buyers have been slow on the uptake – perhaps finding his high energy brand of country music too close to rock'n'roll. Ely's band is held in high esteem by other musicians as amongst the hottest in the business.*

toppers. His success has led the Nashville bosses to forget their anger and to welcome him back with open arms. His new music is now almost as established as the mainstream sounds he was escaping from.

The Willie Nelson success story has run parallel with Jennings's although he now seems to have overtaken the younger singer in terms of popularity. Long acknowledged as one of the greatest country songwriters of all time, Nelson's simple style as a performer ran so against the grain of the contemporary sounds of the Sixties that few believed he could ever be more than a very average country artist selling a few thousand records a year and filling only small concert halls or clubs. But he proved his detractors wrong by becoming the major country music figure of the late Seventies – outselling everyone else.

Nelson moved to Nashville in the Fifties and quickly established his reputation as a songwriter. He worked for a time with fellow Texan Ray Price as a member of his Cherokee Cowboys, then formed his own group. He made many records in the Sixties

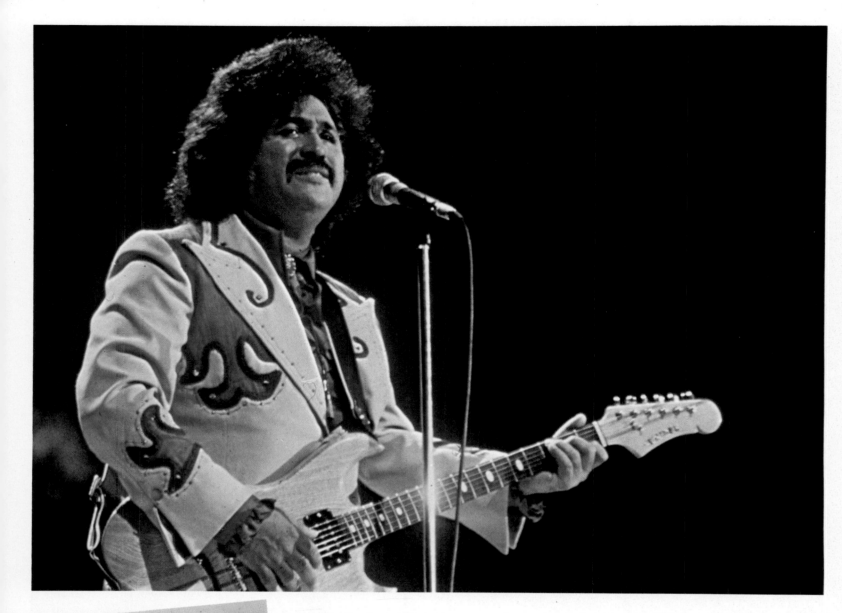

top: *Freddy Fender worked as a musician for twenty years in rough, dingy bars in the Rio Grande Valley and the big cities of Texas and Louisiana before his luck changed when a song he'd recorded called* Before The Next Teardrop Falls *was a major pop and country hit.*

above: *Kinky Friedman, a Texan Jew, is perhaps the most unlikely country singer you're ever likely to hear. His songs about mass murderers, water closets and Jesus would be extremely offensive sung by anyone else but Kinky somehow manages to get away with them.*

but had only moderate success. It was not uncommon for him to record basic tracks then leave them for the producer and engineer to add whatever strings they felt were necessary.

He became increasingly frustrated about the way his records were made and the lack of promotion he was receiving. He hired a lawyer, Neil Reshen, to get him out of his RCA contract and signed with Atlantic and recorded two great albums *Shotgun Willie* and *Phases and Stages* both in a far simpler style than his previous dozen or so releases. Willie then moved to CBS and recorded *The Red Headed Stranger*, an album which included the single *Blue Eyes Crying In The Rain*. The single was a massive crossover hit and meant Willie was finally on his way to national fame and fortune as a performer.

Nelson's house in Nashville burnt down and he moved to Austin. His concerts there drew an extraordinary mixture of hippies and rednecks. His outlaw reputation became firmly established and like-minded musicians from all over the South flocked to the Texas capital to be part of the new movement.

The appeal of Willie Nelson is today even more widespread. 1978's best selling country album was *Stardust* – Nelson's interpretations of standards by Hoagy Carmichael, Irving Berlin and George Gershwin. He continues to tour, still preferring one-night stands to long engagements, and has become involved with TV and films.

Kris Kristofferson is the third Texan who played a vital role in the revolution in styles within Nashville in the Seventies. He wrote brilliant songs that were mature and intelligent without losing the fundamental simplicity and directness of the classic country songs of the past.

He spent four years hanging around Nashville trying to get a break, then in 1969 Roger Miller recorded *Me and Bobby McGee*. Shortly afterwards the song was recorded by Janis Joplin and went to the top of the pop charts. Kris continued to write and signed a recording contract with Columbia that introduced his attractive, growling vocals to the public.

He married singer Rita Coolidge in 1973, his most successful year as a recording artist, and they worked together making records, films and in live shows. From then on his records and songs became less interesting but he has developed into an enormously popular film star.

Kristofferson liberated country music songwriting from its previous restrictions

above: *Waylon Jennings is seen here with his attractive wife Jessi Colter. Born Miriam Johnson in Phoenix she first came to prominence as a songwriter called Miriam Eddy – she was then married to Duane Eddy who had several pop instrumental hits in the early Sixties. Waylon discovered her songs soon after the end of her first marriage, recorded a couple then persuaded her to sing duets with him. He arranged a recording contract for her and she changed her name – she was the great-great-great-grandniece of Jesse Colter, a counterfeiter who had been a member of the infamous outlaw gang led by Jesse James.*

and, because his songs were hits, other writers have been encouraged to follow his lead. Many of the most talented new writers of the Seventies are from Texas. Guy Clark, who has written some classic ballads about old-time Texas – *Desperados Waiting For A Train* and *The Last Gunfighter Ballad*; Rodney Crowell, a former member of Emmylou Harris's Hot Band and composer of some of her best songs; Billy Joe Shaver, who wrote all but one of the tunes on Waylon's *Honky Tonk Heroes*; and Townes Van Zandt whose credits include the saga of *Poncho and Lefty*.

Joe Ely is the most talked about new writer and performer to have come out of Texas in quite a time. Very popular in his home state he has had little success outside – his records are considered too rock for the country radio stations and too country for the rock ones. His band, all from his home town of Lubbock, is among the most talented and exciting of the country acts to be seen live anywhere.

Guy Clark, Rodney Crowell, Billy Joe Shaver and Townes Van Zandt have all had songwriting success but, like Joe Ely, have yet to achieve the popularity as performers they might have hoped for. Like Willie Nelson they may have to wait a long time for country music business people and record buyers to catch up with their special talents.

A word or two finally about the best places to see and hear authentic Texas country

BUDDY HOLLEY   LARRY WELBORN   BOB MONTGOMERY

♪ *Buddy and Bob* ♪
"WESTERN AND BOP"

BUS. MANAGER
HI POCKETS DUNCAN

KDAV BOX 1319
LUBBOCK, TEXAS

music – the honky tonks. For years the name was synonymous with sleazy wooden buildings, rough-edged music, heavy drinking, energetic dancing and wild fights. Things have changed a lot from the days when a musician had to be prepared to use his fists as well as his guitar but the honky tonks that remain are still unpretentious looking places where Texan country fans go to forget their troubles, let their hair down and hear some good music.

The biggest Texas honky tonk is probably Mickey Gilley's famous club in the Houston suburb of Pasadena. Gilley's is wide enough to herd cattle through and one of the best places to go dancing on a Saturday night. Smaller, but equally atmospheric honky tonks can be found in Fort Worth's Cowtown area, Dallas, Austin and Lubbock.

It was in honky tonks that white musicians like Bob Wills and his Texas Playboys brought together the various musical styles of the state and created their own rich brand of music. Texan country stars of today like Willie Nelson grew up in the musical atmosphere of honky tonks and served their apprenticeships in them. It is interesting to speculate that amongst the unknown artists performing today in the honky tonks that remain – venues like the Soap Creek Saloon in Austin, the Longhorn Ballroom in Dallas, and the Cotton Club in Lubbock – there may be a country superstar of the future.

above: *Buddy Holly from Lubbock, Texas was one of the brightest stars of rock'n'roll in the late Fifites but died tragically in an aircrash on 3rd February 1959. His innovative musical sound was strongly rooted in country and has had a lasting influence on rock. The most country-orientated of his recordings that survive are tapes he made with his longtime friend Bob Montgomery in 1954–55 when they were both still at school, but had their own* Buddy and Bob: Western and Bop *show broadcast over a local radio station.*

right: *Cain's Ballroom in Tulsa, Oklahoma, an old-time dance hall still decorated with photos of Bob Wills and other country stars of the Thirties and Forties. Once the home of Wills's radio activities, Tulsa is currently the headquarters of Jim Halsey's music empire.*

I T'S sad but true that talent alone is not enough. No matter how impressive the vocal style a country singer may possess, it is possible, or rather probable, that he or she will never make the grade without the combined help of the various songwriters, arrangers, producers, agents and managers who keep the wheels of the country wagon forever turning. Sometimes, as in the case of Billy Sherrill, producer of Tammy Wynette, George Jones, Barbara Fairchild, Tanya Tucker, Charlie Rich and many others, these people have become almost as well known as those they have helped to prosper. Few country music fans are not aware of producers like Allen Reynolds, Chet Atkins, Shelby Singleton and Jack Clement; arrangers such as Bill Justis and Bergen White; plus a host of fine song-writers including Bob McDill, Dallas Frazier, Harlan Howard, Dennis Linde, Bill Anderson, Hank Cochran, Shel Silverstein, Boudleaux and Felice Bryant, and Tom T. Hall, many of them excellent performers in their own right. But, give or take a Colonel Parker or two, managers and agents tend to remain background figures, content mainly to accept their due percentage and forever push the careers of those they represent.

Jim Halsey, who has been called 'the single most important man in country music', He met Halsey soon after the Kansan set out to fame-push Wanda Jackson. Wanda, an stepped momentarily into the limelight in 1978, when he appeared at Nashville's CMA Awards ceremony to pick up the Manager Of The Year award. There is little doubt that he deserved it. For that same night, Don Williams, then managed by Halsey, had been acclaimed Male Vocalist Of The Year, while Roy Clark, The Oak Ridge Boys and The Oak Ridge Boys Band, all Halsey acts, had scooped the Top Instrumentalist, Best Vocal Group and Best Band plaudits respectively.

A quiet, thoughtful man, Jim Halsey is the very antithesis of the high-powered heavies one usually associates with music management. He moved into the promotion side of entertainment during the Forties when, while still at Independence Junior College, Kansas, he, like his son Sherman today, became a booker, originally signing swing bands, musicals, ice shows – anything that might prove entertaining to a college audience. 'But the one thing I was always successful with was country music,' Halsey remembers. 'Come snow or ice, people would still turn up for that.' Among the acts that he booked was Hank Thompson, who had a massive selling record with *Whoa Babe* in 1949. The two became firm friends and at the end of 1951, Halsey, then 20 years old, became Hank's manager and went on the road. 'I got a portable typewriter and a bag of clothes and simply boarded Hank's bus. I made 250 dates that year – that's where I learned the business. I also learned the geography too – for I'd hardly been out of Kansas at the time.'

Today, Halsey still represents Thompson, along with Roy Clark, Tammy Wynette, Rick Nelson, Jody Miller, Johnny Rodriguez, Freddy Fender, Mel Tillis, The Oak Ridge Boys, Ray Price, Donna Fargo and many other stars whose names have consistently registered on the pop and country charts. Clark, the multi-talented entertainer who has won just about every award a country picker can accrue became in 1973 the first performer to win the country entertainer of the year accolade from the CMA, the Academy of Country Music and the American Guild of Variety Artists in the same year. He met Halsey soon after the Kansan set out to fame-push Wanda Jackson. Wanda, an

TODAY TULSA —TOMORROW THE WORLD

eighteen-year-old bundle of rock from Oklahoma City, signed with Halsey in 1956 and by the early Sixties was logging such hits as *Let's Have A Party*, *Right Or Wrong* and *In The Middle Of A Heartache*. Roy Linwood Clark was her guitarist and banjoist, and an obvious star in his own right – a fact that didn't escape Halsey, who later set out to make the likeable Clark into one of country's highest paid stars. Clark, a fine comedian in addition to being an exceptional instrumentalist and singer, epitomises most of Halsey's acts in that his appeal is far broader than that of most down-the-line country vocalists. This is true, too, of Freddy Fender, Rick Nelson and Tammy Wynette, all artists of international stature, capable of attracting huge audiences wherever they play. Lesser known are The Oak Ridge Boys who used to be a pure gospel group but, under Halsey, have developed a stage act second to none. An energetic band, headed by a manic, cloaked butterball of a keyboardist known simply as Garland, The Oaks rock, sing pop and country and generally leap about the stage with a fervour that has brought them a whole new public. Paul Simon asked them to back him on his *Slip Slidin' Away* single and they have since had hit records of their own. Destined to become even bigger, The Oaks are indicative of Halsey's wide view of country appealing to both young and old. Ray Price is another who fails to conform to the accepted image of a country star – even though he is an established artist with a huge tally of hits that span all the way back to '52. A honky-tonk singer at heart, he appears on stage in a tuxedo, fronting an orchestra that wouldn't disgrace Kostelanetz. Both Opry and Carnegie Hall, he is Halsey's kind of country.

opposite: *Here he's nimble-pickin' on a twelve-string, but Roy Clark can play banjo, fiddle, accordion, piano, trumpet, trombone and drums. He's also a top-flight comedian and a singer whose recording of* Yesterday When I Was Young *became a nationwide Top Twenty hit – which is why he's been voted Entertainer of the Year by both the Country Music Association and the Academy of Country Music. Roy was once a professional boxer who won fifteen straight fights as a light-heavyweight before opting for a musical career.*

above: *Barbara Fairchild, one of the many talented acts on the Halsey roster. In 1972 she topped the country charts with* Teddy Bear, *then followed up with* Kid Stuff *and* Baby Doll *– though by the late Seventies her winning streak seemed to be petering out. 'But life rolls on,' she says philosophically. 'And you gotta go with it or roll right under it!'*

above: *In 1951 Hank Thompson looked around for a manager before remembering a twenty-year-old college booker from Kansas named Jim Halsey. Under Halsey's guidance he began playing non-country dates and big-band ballrooms, in 1957 moving into Las Vegas to appear at the Golden Nugget. It's also claimed that he was the first country performer to record in hi-fi, the first to cut a stereo album and the first to make a live recording. A singer during his US Navy days in the South Pacific, Hank formed his Brazos Valley Boys in the mid-Forties and by 1948 had logged two major hit records in* Humpty Dumpty Heart *and* Today, *the start of a long string of chart successes. Thompson is nowadays not only one of Halsey's leading acts but also the Kansan's business partner.*

Gatemouth Brown is a more recent addition to the Halsey stable – but he conforms with Jim's 'something extra' requirement. A black musician who spent years leading a big band, he dresses like the baddie in an old-time western movie – complete with black stetson – and plays both blues guitar and bluegrass fiddle. He switches style with alacrity which can be confusing for a dyed-in-the-wool country audience! However, his act, which includes a marathon version of *Orange Blossom Special* filled with various impressions created on Gate's fiddle, has proved a show-stopper time and time again. There is little doubt of his entertainment value.

Halsey loves entertainers and knows how to channel their efforts in the most lucrative direction. Mel Tillis was just a good country singer who stuttered before signing to Jim Halsey Inc. To most, Mel's vocal impediment might have been seen as a formidable problem when trying for TV exposure – but not to Halsey. Dick Howard, the company's vice-president and the man in charge of Halsey's TV operations, explains, 'I went to certain talk and game shows and other programmes where they thought Mel's stutter would be uncontrollable and a turn-off to the audience. But I knew it was someting he'd been able to cope with and turn into an asset rather than a liability. So I stuck with it. And, though it took me two years to get him onto *Hollywood Squares* because they were afraid of that stutter, now he's a regular and they're happy to have

him any time he wants to do the show.'

Halsey now works out of Tulsa, where he, Roy Clark and Hank Thompson, who are now his business partners, own radio stations, music publishing firms, an advertising agency and various other business ventures. His penthouse office is staffed by an array of beautiful women – his executive vice-president, Dianna Pugh, is an amazingly efficient blonde whose looks would grace any Hollywood production – and ticks over like the proverbial well-oiled machine. Meanwhile, Halsey continues to push on with his plan for world domination by country music. In 1971 he organized a small party on a ranch just a short way from Tulsa. But, because Halsey *is* Halsey, the annual party became bigger and bigger until it became a country music showcase called the Tulsa International Music Festival, an event which in 1978 attracted some 21,000 people to the shows at the city's Assembly Centre – while Halsey's guest list for the weekend numbered 700, this figure including 400 talent buyers from clubs, country fairs etc., scores of artists and record company executives, plus 142 media representatives from all over the world.

Only by thinking big, Halsey opines, will country music prosper. It has to become increasingly international – which is why, following his ground-breaking country music shows at New York's Carnegie Hall and the placing of many of his acts at leading

above: *An enthusiastic fan embraces Rick Nelson during his performance at the 1978 Tulsa International Music Festival, an event which not only featured Roy Clark, Barbara Fairchild, Donna Fargo, The Oak Ridge Boys, Joe Stampley, Don Williams, Mel Tillis, Jana Jae, Tammy Wynette, Hank Thompson, Ray Price and many, many fine country acts but also included a multi-media laser presentation utilizing twenty slide projectors, four lasers and a sound track fed through a computer. Rick himself is a born-in-a-trunk entertainer, the son of bandleader Ozzie Nelson and vocalist Harriet Hilliard who achieved further fame in the long-running radio and TV series* The Adventures of Ozzie And Harriet. *A teen idol during the late Fifties and early Sixties, Rick has now turned to country.*

right: *The urbane Ray Price, one of country's most successful entertainers. He originally set out to be a vet but later opted for a career in music, forming his band, The Cherokee Cowboys, from the remnants of Hank Williams's Drifting Cowboys. An Opry star in 1952, two years later he began an incredible run of hits that continued through to the end of the Seventies, his tally of chart records including* Crazy Arms, I've Got A New Heartache, My Shoes Keep Walking Back To You, City Lights, Heartaches By The Number, The Same Old Me, One More Time, Soft Rain, Make The World Go Away, Burning Memories, The Other Woman, Touch My Heart, For The Good Times, I Won't Mention It Again, I'd Rather Be Sorry, Lonesome Lonesome, She's Got To Be A Saint, You're The Best Thing, Roses And Love Songs *plus many others. Willie Nelson, Jimmy Day, Buddy Emmons, Roger Miller and Johnny Bush are just a few of the country stars who have appeared in Ray's band throughout the years, though nowadays he fronts an outfit that looks pure Carnegie Hall. Like most Texans, he loves horses almost as much as he loves music and spends much of his time on a ranch.*

opposite: *Art collector and country-music agent Jim Halsey, the first man to sell country sounds to the Soviet Union. Quiet and unassuming, he doesn't smoke, gamble and drinks only wine – but he hosted such marvellous ranch parties that they grew into a whole country festival. In 1979 he set up a new company called Thunderbird Artists in an effort to promote up-and-coming acts and attract fresh audiences to country music. Later he also endeared himself to existing fans by reuniting Tammy Wynette and George Jones for a series of shows – the first time since 1975 that the duo had toured together.*

Las Vegas venues, he exported a show, featuring Roy Clark, The Oaks, banjoist Buck Trent and vocal group Sugah, to Moscow and Leningrad, gaining a glowing tribute in *Pravda:*

> The artists of the Roy Clark Country Show advantageously differ from the idols of vulgar commercial western entertainment, both in repertoire and manner of performance. They represent a special independent trend of easily accessible, popular music – country music – which relies on the centuries-old national traditions . . . The country audience is not a select public of fashionable concert halls of New York and Boston, but rural toilers and workers of the southern 'depths' of America and sometimes even simply passersby . . . Country music preaches broad humanistic ideals – about good and evil, and what should be done so that all people on earth would live under a peaceful sky.

'We've set about a systematic programme to get our artists out into the world,' explains Halsey. 'It's a small place now because there's no transportation problem any more. The music is being accepted because of television – there's so much television and radio that encompasses country music – and by doing all these personal appearances we're helping to create a whole new market.' Jim's systematic programme has been in operation for a few months now.

During that time, The Oaks have played a number of performances at London's Albert Hall, Roy Clark and Don Williams have headed the first-ever Country Music Gala at the prestigious Midem Festival at Cannes, and dates have been lined up for Halsey's heroes in Europe, Japan, Australia, New Zealand and the Phillipines. It is not, though, just wide-appeal artists in which Halsey is interested (he hates the use of the term 'crossover act') or the provision of countless new venues. For he wants country music shows to compete on the same level as the more elaborate rock concerts, offering light shows and lasers, dry ice and other trappings.

'The rock people have been doing this for years,' he points out. 'They're in show business just like the Ringling Brothers and Barnum & Bailey . . . and so are we. One thing though - I insist on everything being done in good taste.' He insists, of course, in his own quiet way. Insists and persists. And by this sheer persistence he makes country music grow.

FIRST time visitors to Nashville are often puzzled – and disappointed – when they pay a visit to the famous 'Music Row' – 16th and 17th Avenues and the streets that link them. Expecting tall, impressive buildings bearing the logos of RCA, Capitol and the other record labels of their favourite country singers they find instead a couple of remarkably ordinary looking streets comprising mostly two-storey houses – some private residences, others converted into offices – a handful of bars, a doss-house and some plain looking modern buildings.

This *is* where the studios, record company offices and publishing houses are located but the area is very dull for tourists and there is very little of interest for photographers. Sharp-eyed fans who are prepared to wait around for a few hours might catch a glimpse of a famous face or two because the area is, not surprisingly, overflowing with talented people, but a glimpse is about all they can hope for because the polite but firm young ladies at the reception desks of record companies or studios rarely let anyone past them unless they are on official business.

The best place for country fans to go from here is to the junction of 16th Avenue, Division and Demonbreun Streets where there are a number of souvenir shops, a wax museum, the starting-points of bus tours on 'The Homes of the Stars' route and, best of all, The Country Music Hall of Fame and Museum. A new building standing proudly at the very beginning of Music Row, it resembles a modern church and is Nashville's shrine to country music. A visit here will more than compensate for any disappointment suffered in the nearby business area – it is full of sights and sounds that bring to life great moments from the past: films photographs, stage costumes, musical instruments and fascinating collections of memorabilia – it is an ideal place to learn more about country music.

The Country Music Foundation, which is responsible for looking after the building, was created in 1964 with the specific aim of creating a museum and library devoted to country music. The original was opened in 1967 but a newly re-modelled and expanded museum was opened in 1977. It incorporates several exhibits, displays being periodically changed and modified, and at least one completely new exhibit is created every year. This ensures that every time you visit there is something different to see – it also means that a description like this one may well include something that will not be on display when you visit.

Once inside many people head for the small movie theatre where short films are shown that give life again to dearly loved performers who have died, like Jim Reeves, Bob Wills and his Texas Playboys. Very popular are showings of the rare short *The Singing Brakeman* which features Jimmie Rodgers performing *Waiting For A Train*, *Daddy and Home* and *T For Texas*.

There are cases of memorabilia from several country music personalities and you can find everything from Opry comic Minnie Pearl's original straw hat (complete with price tag) and Patsy Cline's cigarette lighter – retrieved from the wreckage of her plane crash – which is decorated with a confederate flag and plays *Dixie* when opened.

Country music's evolution during three hundred years is traced in a number of exhibits but is best illustrated in the art gallery's large mural by Thomas Hart Benton

THE COUNTRY MUSIC HALL OF FAME

above: *The museum contains the Country Artists' Touring Bus – an impressive vehicle though somewhat lacking in special features when compared to Conway Twitty's remarkable automobile shown here with the singer aboard. Like many other country stars, Conway tours extensively throughout the USA and for much of the year the bus is his home. It has a sophisticated hi-fi system, cooking facilities, comfortable seating and sleeping accommodation.*

called *The Sources of Country Music*. Benton, a highly respected Missouri artist who was also a musician, was commissioned to paint a mural that would depict the important musical and cultural traditions of country. The Anglo-American folk cultures are illustrated by pioneer fiddlers, square dancers, ballad singers with dulcimers and white spiritualists singing hymns. The Afro-American influence is depicted with a blues singer. There is a singing cowboy demonstrating the importance of western themes in the music and a riverboat and a train, familiar subjects in so many country songs.

The history of musical instruments used by folk and country musicans over the last three centuries is traced in a museum exhibit entitled *Tools of Music*. The earliest on display are the authentic folk instruments – dulcimers, fiddles and banjos. The fiddle, the smallest and highest pitched member of the violin family, came to America with the

above right: *After the Grand Ole Opry, Nashville's most important tourist attraction is the Country Music Hall of Fame which stands at 4 Music Square East at the head of Music Row. The museum pays homage to the greats of country music, presenting its history in a series of audio-visual montages, collections of rare and valuable instruments and memorabilia.*

earliest settlers and was to be the most important instrument for folk and country musicians until comparatively recently. Most country bands in the Twenties were led by the fiddle while guitars and banjos played a supporting role but by the late Thirties guitars had taken over.

The original dulcimer, an instrument comprising several wires that were struck with wooden hammers (a forerunner of the piano), was very popular in mountain communities in the seventeenth century but later lost favour as its fragility and its lack of volume made it unsuitable for public performances. The Appalachian dulcimer, a smaller instrument with just a few strings that are plucked rather than struck, is of later origin and while not as popular as the banjo, fiddle or guitar, is still used by some folk and traditional country outfits.

People often describe the banjo as America's only native instrument, but it seems likely that the instrument – which looks like a cross between a small drum and a guitar – was derived from an African instrument called a Banjar and was first brought to America by African slaves. The original banjo had four strings but during the nineteenth century in Virginia a fifth was added and an instrument was created that was ideally suited to accompany vocals in traditional folk music. The revolutionary change caused by adding the new string meant that musicians had to invent new ways of playing it. The banjo had lost a lot of its popularity by the 1920s but bluegrass musicians in the Forties led a revival of interest that continues today.

The museum offers considerable space to the guitar which is now the pre-eminent instrument in country music. Its importance in terms of country music is a recent occurrence. It replaced the fiddle in the Thirties but its position was considerably strengthened when rock'n'roll musicians, many of whom had come from country

left: *The plaques and portraits in the Country Music Hall of Fame pay tribute to the most revered figures in country music's history. Kitty Wells, the Queen of Country Music, was elected in 1976.*

above: *The great Hank Williams was one of the first to be honoured with a place in the Country Music Hall of Fame, in 1961. His plaque reads: 'The simple, beautiful melodies and straightforward plaintive stories in his lyrics of life as he knew it will never die.'*

top: *It shouldn't be long before Earl Scruggs joins the luminaries in the Hall of Fame. With Lester Flatt he has done much to popularise bluegrass music and pioneered the three-finger style of banjo-playing now used by musicians throughout the world.*

backgrounds, ensured it was the main instrument in pop music as well. Two guitars, a Gibson Les Paul electric and a Gallagher acoustic, have been 'exploded' to show how they were built. Nearby are a collection of some rare and famous guitars, including Gene Autrey's Martin 00–42 and Elvis Presley's Martin D–18 which he used on his earliest tours and for the historic Sun recording sessions in Memphis, Tennessee in the mid-Fifties.

Elvis Presley is remembered elsewhere in the museum's most impressive and popular exhibit. His custom-made 'solid gold' 1960 Cadillac – presented by Elvis, the Colonel and RCA Records just three months before the singer's death – stands gleaming impressively at one end of a room, the roof having been neatly cut back to reveal an interior where everything is gold – a record player, a bar, a brush and comb set, a TV set (though with a black-and-white picture) and, of course, gold records.

Next to this fantasy car is a section of another musician's vehicle – less exceptional but more functional. 'The Country Music Artist's Touring Bus' shows the various customised features that many artists have had installed in their travelling homes. The quality of the special features obviously varies with the earning power of individual artists but most have bunks so that musicians can sleep on the journeys between shows that often last many hours, tables where they can eat or play card games, radios, tape players, CB radios and (for some) video-cassette televisions. These special facilities help time pass more quickly than it would in more conventional touring vehicles where there is little to do except sit and watch the endless ribbon of highway.

At the heart of the museum is the Hall of Fame where there are bronze plaques and portraits of the illustrious members. Hall of Fame members are voted by a committee of one hundred from the Country Music Foundation and one or more new members are elected each year. The first six were Ernest Tubb, Roy Acuff, Tex Ritter, Jimmie Rodgers, Hank Williams and Fred Rose. Today the numbers have swelled to around thirty of the most important people in country music's history. Their numbers include influential musicians like The Original Carter Family, Bob Wills and Bill Monroe, executives like Stephen Sholes and a few people who are both – like Chet Atkins super-picker and RCA executive.

Nashville's Hall of Fame and Museum is a fine monument to country music and its rich heritage, and anyone lucky enough to visit 'Music City' should make sure they pay it a visit.

'They used to call me rockabilly,
All of us ran through.
Then Elvis opened up the door,
Doo Wop A Bop Bam Boo.'
I Will Rock And Roll With You Johnny Cash

BLACK music and country have always gone hand in hand. Jimmie Rodgers, heavily influenced by black musicians, cut a succession of high-selling blues discs during his career, while during the Thirties and Forties, western swing bands copied countless riffs of Ellington, Henderson, Basie and other black swing stars, reshaping them in a way that made them just that bit more palatable to the audiences of Texas and Oklahoma. Nobody ever mentioned the word crossover. And nobody thought it in the least odd that a trumpet or sax solo on the black jukebox record should be transformed into a fiddle or steel guitar feature on the western swing cover version. Things just happened that way, dividing lines becoming so blurred that they often disappeared altogether – which they did when Hank Williams eventually made his way onto the scene. Williams, a rebel, an alcoholic and a pill addict, wrote the kind of songs that bridged generation gaps and broke down racial barriers. An Alabama born country singer who had learnt his music from a black street singer named Tee-Tot, Hank sang *Move It On Over*, a 1948 forerunner of *Rock Around The Clock*, and a new kind of youth-oriented music burst into life. Williams's life was brief – by New Year's Day, 1953, he was dead, the supposed victim of a heart-attack while on his way to a gig in Canton, Ohio. A few months later, his *Weary Blues From Waitin'* entered the charts – his 28th hit record in less than five years.

Though few realised it, the waiting was over. A country band named The Saddlemen had already elected to become Bill Haley And The Comets, while down in Memphis, Elvis Presley, an employee of the Crown Electric Company, could be heard whistling hillbilly tunes as he drove one of the company's brace of trucks along the highway. Haley had always been country. He had worked with such bands as The Downhomers, The Texas Range Riders and The Four Aces Of Western Swing. In 1952 he tried a new angle and recorded a version of *Rocket 88*, a song penned by a rhythm and blues singer, Jackie Brenston, following this with a number of similar recordings for the Essex label. One of these, *Crazy, Man, Crazy*, climbed into the national Top 20 and from that moment on, it seemed that all hell had been let loose. Oddly enough, Haley offered little that hadn't been around for years. He had merely added a jumped-up hillbilly beat (later known as rockabilly) to the R&B sound pioneered by Louis Jordan's Tympany Five in the Forties – even recreating *Ch-Choo-Chboogie*, a 1946 Jordan hit. But to the youth of the world, Haley's music was a rebel call. When he appeared in the film *Rock Around The Clock*, they broke the cinema seats and danced in the aisles.

Rockabilly itself was nothing new. It had grown out of western swing and had become a hit sound in the hands of Tennessee Ernie Ford in the late Forties and early Fifties, who provided an amalgam of boogie and country that had the nation bopping to such discs as *Smokey Mountain Boogie* and *Shotgun Boogie*. But Ford was too old to become a teenage idol – and Haley, though initially hailed as one, was equally

ROCK AND THE COUNTRY CONNECTION

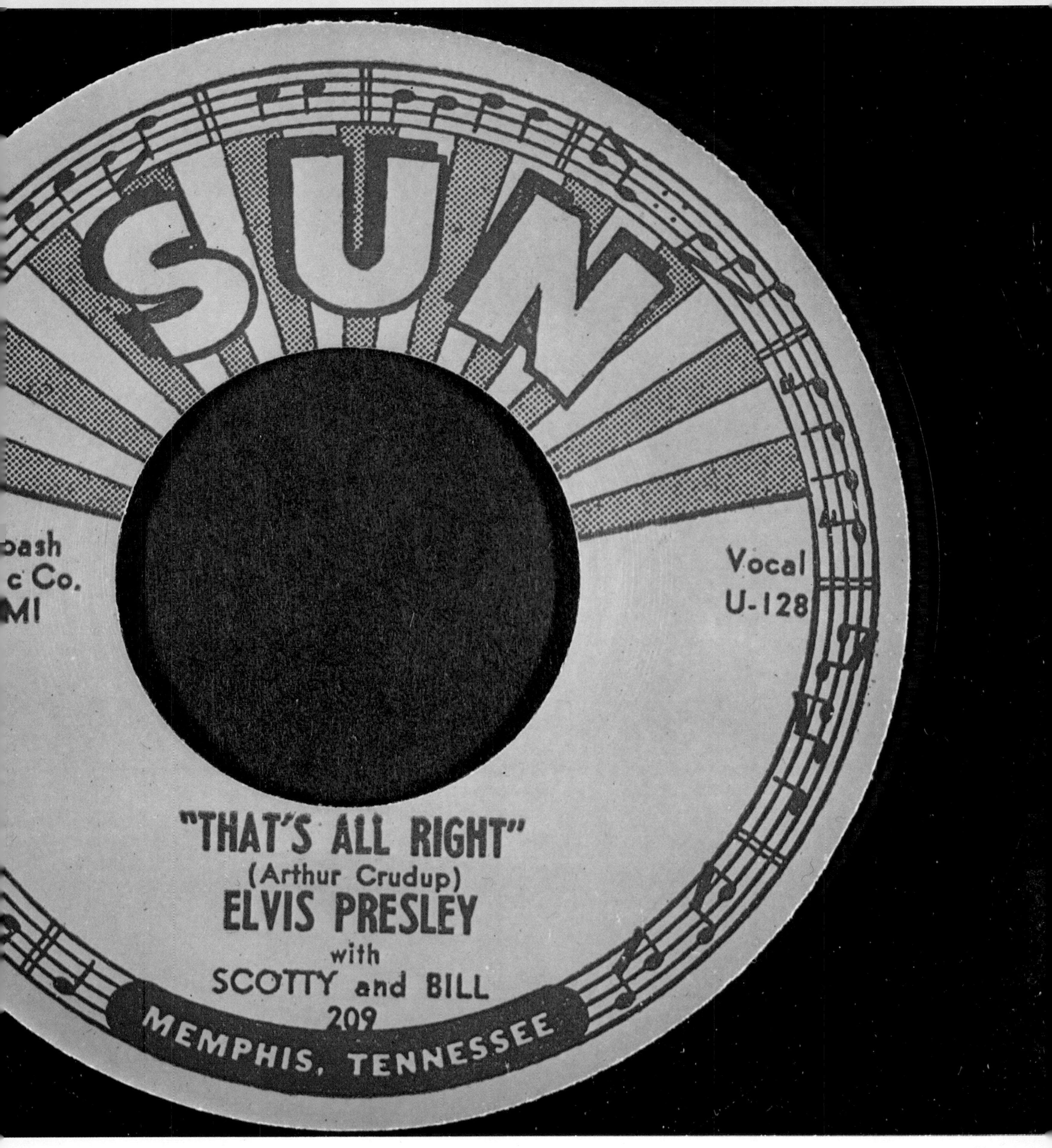

unsuitable age-wise. And so it was that Elvis Presley, dark, handsome and only nineteen, stepped forward at just the right moment and was duly crowned as king. He too was pure country. His first recordings included versions of Bill Monroe's *Blue Moon Of Kentucky* and Jim Reeves's *I Love You Because,* his first major tour was with Hank Snow's Jamboree, while some of his earliest broadcasts were with the Louisiana Hayride. But, like Jimmie Rodgers and Hank Williams before him, Elvis had a feel for black music. So he included bluesman Big Boy Crudup's *That's All Right Mama* on his initial date for Sun Records and had it released as his first single. Once more, the mixture of black music and country worked – and Elvis duly took his place in rock history, though he never forgot his roots, always featuring some country material in his stage act and on recording dates.

Presley's rise to fame inspired a large number of country hopefuls to set their sights on the rock market. Jerry Lee Lewis, a frantic keyboardist given to climbing on top of the piano in mid-act; Don and Phil Everly, who offered nasal duets on top of a highly produced background sound; Buddy Holly, a singer who hiccoughed his way to fame and posthumous adulation – all made the switch from country to rock with considerable success, Jerry Lee came from Louisiana and was initially influenced by honky-tonk man Moon Mullican; Don and Phil were the sons of country singers Ike and Margaret Everly; Holly once formed a 'western bop' duo with producer Bob Montgomery; and other rockers such as Charlie Rich, Carl Perkins, Charlie Feathers and even Brenda Lee all came with a modicum of country in their soul, finding acceptance with an audience that normally associated country entertainers with hayseed, hoedowns and hi-y'all.

Elvis apart, few maintained the pace. Basic rock 'n' roll became *passé* for a new generation of youth, who were looking for something a trifle more sophisticated. And in the Sixties as the Beatles edged their way towards electronic gimmickry and such bands as Pink Floyd opted for psychedelic flights of fancy, Jerry Lee, The Everlys, Conway Twitty, Waylon Jennings, Ricky Nelson and many other first generation rockers either turned or returned to country and a hopefully more stable existence. It was Twitty, who had been born Harold Lloyd Jenkins and fashioned his pseudonym from the names of two towns (Conway, in Arkansas, and Twitty, in Texas) that made the most spectacular switch. A massive seller of pop records during the late Fifties and early Sixties – his 1958 recording of *It's Only Make Believe* sold over four million copies and remained in the charts for 21 weeks – Twitty, who had formerly led a country band named The Cimarrons during his army service in Japan, virtually faded from the best-selling lists by 1963. Three years later he returned to country music and began an incredible run of hits – most of them reaching the coveted No. 1 spot – that continues to the present day.

But not only failed rockers moved into country. Many young musicians looking for a different peg on which to hang their musical hats, discovered that a combination of rock and country could not only prove aesthetically satisfying but could also appeal to a whole new audience. Among the first to make some impact were the brothers

above left: *Carl Perkins and Johnny Cash. The son of a poor Tennessee farmer, Perkins first played in honky tonks and small halls with his brothers Jay and Clayton. After a short stay with Flip Records, he began recording with Sam Phillips's Sun label in 1955, his second release being* Blue Suede Shoes, *a smash hit later covered by Elvis Presley. However, in March 1956, he was involved in a car crash which killed his brother Jay and left Carl with multiple injuries, thus taking him out of the race to the top.*

Rodney and Doug Dillard, who came from a family with a long tradition in bluegrass music. After playing the coffee house circuit for a while, they signed with Elektra Records in 1963 and became popular on the flourishing folk scene. Also around this time The Hillmen, another bunch of up-and-comers formed by mandolinist Chris Hillman and the guitar and bass playing Gosdin Brothers, began recording a bluegrass album in California. And it was from these two units that a major proportion of the whole country-rock family tree was to evolve, Hillman going on to become a founder member of the Byrds, the band that changed the whole way of things with *Sweetheart Of The Rodeo*, the first major country-rock album, while Doug Dillard became involved in Dillard and Clark and The Expedition, the last named finally becoming Country Gazette. *Sweetheart Of The Rodeo*, which contained songs penned by Woody Guthrie, the Louvin Brothers and Merle Haggard, was given shape after Gram Parsons, another seminal country-rock figure, joined the ever-changing ranks of the Byrds. Born Cecil Connor, the ill-fated Parsons (he died at the age of 26 from a heart attack caused by a mixture of drink and drugs) was another who first plied his

above: *Nudie, the outrageous Hollywood designer, who has supplied western apparel not only to John Wayne and heroes of many silver-screen sagebrush epics but also to Nashville legends and West Coast country-rockers. Seen with him here is the ill-fated Gram Parsons who, along with the rest of the Flying Burrito Brothers, had a penchant for Nudie suits.*

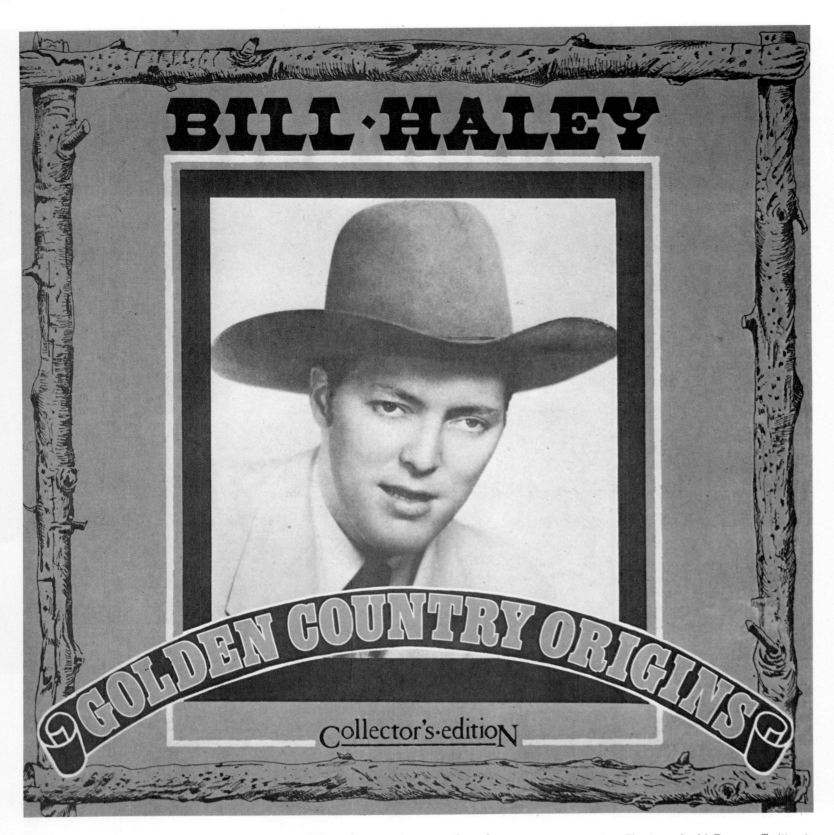

BILL · HALEY

GOLDEN COUNTRY ORIGINS

Collector's edition

trade on the folk scene, later leading a group of West Coast country-rockers known as The International Submarine Band. His stay with the Byrds coincided with a particularly turbulent period of that band's ever stormy evolution and he, in the company of Chris Hillman, quit after just four months in order to form The Flying Burrito Brothers, a fine band with a penchant for dressing in elaborate cowboy gear, embroidered with marijuana leaves, designed by Nudie of Hollywood.

Sartorial misfits they may have been, at least in the world of rock – but musically they were superb, Bob Dylan naming the Burritos as his favourite band in a *Rolling Stone* interview, claiming, 'Boy, I really love them, their records really knock me out.'

Dylan himself had often nodded in the direction of country, using Nashville studios and employing such musicians as Charlie McCoy, Kenny Buttrey, Hargus Robbins and Pete Drake – and in 1969 he provided the final accolade cutting *Nashville Skyline*, a heavily country-oriented album that included a duet with Johnny Cash, who also provided the sleeve poem. A massive seller that included such hit singles as *Lay, Lady, Lay, Tonight I'll Be Staying Here With You* and *I Threw It All Away*, the album provided country with a new respectability. Suddenly it became accepted by those who had sworn allegiance to progressive or underground rock, a fraternity who had formerly considered the genre to be cowboy music – the kind of thing Roy Rogers warbled in B-movies or Frankie Laine sang over the credits of western epics.

opposite: *The 'new look' Conway Twitty at the Wembley Festival of 1979 – for many years he retained the 'greaser' image of the Fifties.*

above: *An album containing country songs recorded by Bill Haley in the years 1948 and 1949. Though now regarded as a rocker, Haley, like Elvis, was a country singer for many years, his first western band being The Texas Range Riders, an outfit that played for birthday parties, community functions and Saturday night get-togethers in the little town of Boothwyn, Pennsylvania. He initially recorded for the Cowboy and Essex labels, cutting such material as Ten Gallon Stetson and Tennessee Border before moving on to Essex Records and finding rock fame with Crazy, Man, Crazy.*

Since then, the growth of 'new country' has accelerated at a tremendous rate, such bands as Area Code 615 (formed from the musicians who played on *Skyline*), Barefoot Jerry, The Eagles, The Ozark Mountain Daredevils, Poco, Dr Hook, Asleep At The Wheel, Mike Nesmith's First National and Countryside Bands, The Amazing Rhythm Aces and scores of others adding their respective chapters to the music's history.

Today it is often hard to differentiate between rock and country music. Musicians who appear at a rock festival one day, are likely to play the Opry on the next. Thankfully, the tasty cocktail that is country-rock is still being stirred – The Nitty Gritty Dirt Band have cut *Will The Circle Be Unbroken*, a marvellous album which also features the talents of Jimmy Martin, Roy Acuff, Merle Travis and the late Mother Maybelle Carter; Ringo Starr and Paul McCartney have both recorded discs in Nashville (The Beatles recorded *Nobody's Child*, a Hank Snow hit, back in their Hamburg days, later adding Johnny Russell's *Act Naturally* to their *Help!* album); Eric Clapton has appeared on stage with Don Williams; Willie Nelson has worked in cahoots with Leon Russell to produce one of his biggest selling albums; and ace five-string banjoist Earl Scruggs seems to have played with just about everybody, once cutting an album which contained contributions from Bob Dylan, Joan Baez, The Byrds and a bluegrass-playing Moog synthesizer! Meanwhile, rockabillies like Mac Curtis, Charlie Feathers and Sleep LaBeef continue to offer age-old acts formed from hot rock and country ballads, while even such easy-listening country acts as Marty Robbins and Roy Clark remember to slip the occasional rock'n'roll item into otherwise straight-forward performances.

Then, of course, there is Hank Snow, the veteran performer who once headed ACE, an organization geared to keeping country music untainted by pop influences. In 1977, aged 63, Hank went into a studio and cut his hundred and fourth album, as rocking an affair as any to emanate from Nashville that year. Like old Hank, country music keeps movin' on. And though it rocks today, tomorrow it may be doing something entirely different.

opposite top: 'The Killer' – piano-pumpin' Jerry Lee Lewis from Ferriday, Louisiana. Originally a country pianist whose style owed much to that of Moon Mullican, Jerry Lee soon latched on to a more frantic approach and began to rival Little Richard. The result was a succession of classic rock'n'roll records plus a blaze of publicity that often worked against him – Lewis getting booed offstage in Britain during 1958, following press reports of his marriage to a 13-year-old child bride. A proud but unpredictable personality, Jerry Lee has always flavoured his act with a high percentage of country material – much to the dismay of his rock'n'roll fans.

opposite bottom: A fine country-rock band, The Amazing Rhythm Aces rose to prominence in 1975 when their recording of Third Rate Romance, *penned by band-member Russell Smith, became a national Top 20 hit.*

above: The Everlys during the rock and rolling heyday. Raised on country music, they became rock idols but remembered their roots when times got hard. By the late Seventies, Don had reverted to being a pure country singer, signing with Roy Acuff's Hickory label.

right: *Barbara Mandrell, yet another country superstar who was born in Texas, comes from a talented musical family and while still a child had become a proficient musician playing steel guitar, bass, banjo and saxophone as well as singing.*

COUNTRY music today is experiencing a new and ubiquitous popularity. In America there are more country radio stations, more country records sold, more country stars appearing on peak-time television, more films using country music themes and soundtracks, and the biggest concert halls in the major cities are putting up Standing Room Only notices at country shows. As we advance through the Eighties there is every indication that the demand for country music will continue to grow.

Considerable growth and expansion can be expected as traditional American music is exported abroad. Just as country music's themes changed and became more relevant to urban Americans as well as rural dwellers in the Sixties they are now proving to have an even more far-reaching appeal. Country music has long been popular in England and the pattern of its growing following there in the last ten years is already beginning to be repeated in other European countries and even in the Far East. In fact, Japan and Germany now put out reissues of old recordings which are simply not available elsewhere.

In England the biggest country acts are those who have made personal appearances in concert and on television. British favourites include Americans long past their peak of popularity in the US but who have spent considerable time and energy courting their British fans, while some of America's most popular country stars are little known because they have never paid the UK a visit. This is well illustrated by the astonishing success of Slim Whitman and the relative failure, to date, of Waylon Jennings. Whitman, a major star of the Fifties in the US, continues to fill the largest British concert halls and his records frequently make the top ten album chart (on one famous occasion a Slim Whitman album came into the charts at number one!) while Waylon, an American superstar, sells few records, never having performed in the UK.

Country music's rapid growth in England in the Seventies owed a lot to television and a big annual festival. There is now at least one country music show every fortnight on British television and albums by Kenny Rogers, Don Williams, Billie Jo Spears and Slim Whitman have all made the top ten following TV advertising campaigns. The cavernous Wembley Arena, located in an outer London suburb, is the venue for an annual International Country Festival which began in 1969 as a one-day event but expanded to two, then three and now four days during the Easter holiday period when it attracts upwards of 40,000 British country fans to see American and English artists.

Festival promoter Mervyn Conn has watched country music's popularity grow year by year in England and is now confident of the same happening in Europe. He has begun promoting festivals in Sweden, Finland, Norway and Germany and his success there has encouraged him to look further afield. The growth in the popularity of the music is evident in record stores in the major European cities – once American country records could only be found in specialist shops but now they are widely displayed in most conventional retail outlets.

The pattern of American artists touring and then reaping healthy record sales afterwards is being repeated in many countries including Japan, one of the world's largest markets for albums. Visits by bluegrass musicians like Bill Monroe, steel guitarists such as Buddy Emmons and crossover stars like Crystal Gayle have

MOVING ON

encouraged a number of local musicians to play country styles. Tokyo has half a dozen country music venues where local performers dressed in American clothes sing American songs in impeccable American accents! Japan's most popular country singers include Noboru Morishita – who covers the songs of Merle Haggard, Marty Robbins, Conway Twitty and Waylon Jennings – and Alice Watanabe – who covers Dolly Parton, Linda Ronstadt and Olivia Newton John.

Like most Japanese singers, the British country artists were once content to merely mimic their American heroes but several are now setting their sights higher and recording their own material in their own styles. Poacher, a six-piece band from the Lancashire town of Warrington; The Bottle City Rockets, a combination of experienced country and rockabilly performers; Chas and Dave, a couple of musicians from London's East End who combine cockney humour with old time rock 'n' roll and country to form a blend of music they term 'rockney'; and solo singers Stu Stevens and Wes McGhee, all have the talent and ambition to find audiences beyond their native shores. It is too early to tell if they will succeed but their determination and

above: *The popularity of singer/songwriter Larry Gatlin has grown year by year and he seems destined to be one of the major stars of the Eighties. He began his musical career with his two brothers and a sister in the family gospel band, The Gatlins, playing the southern states including his native Texas. Dottie West helped him to get his songs published and Kris Kristofferson was instrumental in getting him a solo record contract. His 1976 hit* Broken Lady *served to establish him with country fans in the US and England.*

above right: *Most country artists in Europe please local fans with competent re-workings of country standards, but a few write and record original material. Wes McGhee, who records in a studio in the attic of his North London home, is amongst the best of the new breed who are likely to challenge the American monopoly of the country charts before long.*

professionalism – of a kind not seen from British country artists before – suggests that a UK-based band or singer will begin to find a foothold in the North American domination of country music in the not-too-distant future. Once that has happened the precedent will have been set for musicians from other countries to do the same.

Traditional country artists are very popular with the hard core country fans in Europe and Japan but, as in the US, the big sales are to pop fans buying records by crossover artists. Many country music traditionalists view the effect of crossovers on the future of country music with considerable concern. Leading country music figure and publisher, Wesley Rose, went into print in the music trade paper *Billboard* to express his fears. 'The country music industry is strong and continues to grow, but it is splintering because we have too many artists, producers and record companies thinking "crossover". A really great country record crosses over because of the type of record it is. You don't have to bend over backwards to put hundreds of strings and saxophones on it.'

Many country fans think, like Rose, that country music is in danger of becoming bland and indistinguishable from pop, and they do what they can to discourage crossover acts. In the last few years there has been something of a reversal in this trend and traditional country stars have enjoyed their greatest chart success for a decade or more – this has happened with Ernest Tubb (who spent part of the Seventies without a record label), Kitty Wells, Hank Thompson and Charlie Louvin – while a number of young artists have experienced considerable success with a policy of 'keeping it country'. Their number includes Moe Bandy, who sings in a style strongly influenced by the honky tonk music of the Forties and Fifties, and who has had chart-topping success both as a solo performer and as part of a duo with Joe Stampley. He, however, is grateful for the progress made by the crossover artists for, as he explains, 'Crossover opened the door to bring a lot of pop fans into liking country music in the first place – it exposed people to our sound and to older artists as well.'

DJs and managers of country music radio stations seem to share this view. In 1953 there was just one full-time country radio station – KDAV in Lubbock, Texas – but by 1961 (according to statistics supplied by the Country Music Association in Nashville) there were 81, by 1969 the number had risen to 605 – mainly in the Southern states – but today there are over 1,200, found all over the USA and broadcasting a combined total of about 28,000 hours of country music every day.

Don Langford of the highly successful Los Angeles country station KLAC told *Billboard* magazine a few weeks after Wesley Rose's criticism of artists and producers who have joined the crossover bandwagon, 'Listenership on this station has grown younger during the last ten years. We have that core that's grown up with the music but there's also a segment that has turned to country because of people like Waylon, Willie and Kenny Rogers. They tune in to hear them and then stay with the station.'

Country music has captured the ears of a large proportion of the 25 to 45 age range and crossover artists can take much of the credit. A few years ago this age group would have listened to middle-of-the-road stations that played the music of Tony Bennett, Frank Sinatra and the like but increasingly the trend is towards country and in the future the popularity of country radio stations is likely to be even greater.

Spotting the new and up-and-coming artists who are going to be big in the Eighties and heard on all the country stations, is a difficult, almost impossible task because there are so many talented newcomers around. But we can spotlight a number of young, and not so young, artists who have been showing considerable potential in the last few years and certainly deserve greater success in the future. They can be loosely grouped into three categories: singers using traditional styles, the crossover seekers, and the new outlaws, the successors of Kris Kristofferson and others.

Providing reassurance for the hard core country fans are singers like Gene Watson. With his tear-stained ballads, he has progressed from local record labels in his native Houston to a national deal with Capitol and a handful of hits (so far) including *Paper Rosie*; Vern Gosdin who has had a long career in music, including doing a lot of guitar work on many of the country rock albums produced on the West Coast in the early Seventies, but who is now pursuing a solo career with Elektra Records; Stella Parton with her girl-next-door image that is very different from her big sister Dolly; and The

opposite: Guitarist and singer Ry Cooder was once a highly-paid session musician but now devotes his time to unearthing neglected old songs – folk, country or blues – and restyling them in his own distinctive way. He is a master of his craft and can take the credit for introducing many worthy, but obscure music forms – like the Tex-Mex music of the American born Mexicans in southern Texas – to a wider pop audience.

above Poacher are one of Britain's most successful country bands. They formed in 1977 taking their name from a public house in Winstanley in north-west England. In little more than a year they had made an impact on the all-important American market playing a successful gig at Jim Halsey's annual festival in Tulsa and scoring in the country charts with the hit single Darlin'.

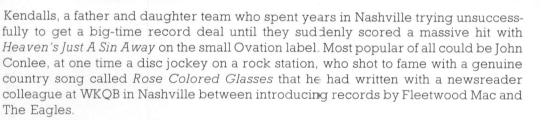

Kendalls, a father and daughter team who spent years in Nashville trying unsuccessfully to get a big-time record deal until they suddenly scored a massive hit with *Heaven's Just A Sin Away* on the small Ovation label. Most popular of all could be John Conlee, at one time a disc jockey on a rock station, who shot to fame with a genuine country song called *Rose Colored Glasses* that he had written with a newsreader colleague at WKQB in Nashville between introducing records by Fleetwood Mac and The Eagles.

Hoping for success in the pop-orientated field are Dave and Sugar who won a lot of fans through several tours supporting Charlie Pride. They have had some big country hits but have yet to break into the pop charts. Great things are predicted for Janie Fricke (pronounced *Frick-ee*) who provided the background vocals for over sixty country hits and worked on Elvis Presley's very last session. She received no public recognition until she was double-billed with Johnny Duncan whom she had helped on a number of hits. She has been carefully groomed by CBS and Billy Sherrill for major success in the future as a solo singer and has, in fact, already had country hits. Con Hunley mixes a number of styles including country, blues, rock 'n' roll, bluegrass and honky-tonk into a commercial blend that suggests he could be as successful a crossover artist as Ronnie Milsap.

The up-and-coming artists in the outlaw mould include songwriters who were involved in the early success of Willie, Waylon and the rest. Billy Joe Shaver has written several of Waylon's best loved songs and has recently made a determined effort to succeed as a singer. Lee Clayton wrote *Ladies Love Outlaws*, the song that launched and named the outlaw movement – his is an original talent and his two Capitol albums are unique both musically and lyrically, comprising songs of raw emotional power and beauty. Like Lee Clayton, the records of James Talley (Jimmy Carter's favourite singer/songwriter) are considered too serious and radical for most country radio stations and therefore don't sell well – yet both artists are amongst the most critically acclaimed singers and writers in country music.

The oldest of the up-and-coming artists is Bobby Bare, who had his first hit in the late Fifties. He was in many ways the original outlaw as the first artist to demand, and get, creative control of his career, and was an important influence and support to many artists, though he has yet to achieve the major star status he has long deserved. A new contract with CBS will hopefully revitalise his career soon. Bare has an ear for the unexpected and was among the first to recognise the talents of Kris Kristofferson and

top: *The Charlie Daniels Band, pictured in front of the House of Commons in London, first came to light in the early Seventies with country and rock fans. They soon found themselves among the front runners of the progressive rock movement of the South along with The Allman Brothers, Marshall Tucker and Lynryd Skynryd, though their music was much more country and bluegrass-biased than any of their contemporaries.*

above: *Mike Nesmith went from being a member of the somewhat bogus mid-Sixties made-for-TV group, The Monkees, to making quality country rock records and writing outstanding songs.*

Waylon Jennings. He recently predicted great things for a young writer and performer called Don Schlitz whose biggest credit to date has been as writer of the award-winning song *The Gambler*.

Country music today is full of people of all ages with a variety of different ideas about the music and how it should be developed. There is an abundance of talent to put these ideas into practice and ensure that country continues to grow and prosper. Crossover artists have brought country music to the attention of an enormous, money-spending audience, who like what they've heard. Some of these artists may well abandon their country roots altogether as many purists have long feared, but there remain plenty of young and talented artists who are still concerned and capable of performing in traditional styles. Country music is alive and thriving and it is assured of a very bright future ahead.

above: *Kris Kristofferson broke numerous Nashville rules in the early Seventies, with his innovative songwriting talents and unconventional appearance; and his success provided inspiration for young writers like Rodney Crowell, Guy Clark and Lee Clayton. A chance meeting with Johnny Cash in Nashville seems to have given him the motivation to come to Music City in 1965 and try his luck as a country songwriter. He is pictured here with country rock singer Rita Coolidge whom he married in 1973. Rita is one of a mere handful of successful singers who were actually born in the country music capital Nashville, Tennessee.*